Contents

Department of Education and Science
HMI Series: Matters for Discussion

Gifted Children in Middle and Comprehensive Secondary Schools

A discussion paper by a working party of
Her Majesty's Inspectorate

London: Her Majesty's Stationery Office

The publications in this series are intended to stimulate professional discussion. They are based on HM Inspectors' observation of work in educational institutions and present their thoughts on some of the issues involved. The views expressed are those of the authors and are not necessarily those of the Inspectorate as a whole or of the Department of Education and Science. It is hoped that they will promote debate at all levels so that they can be given due weight when educational developments are being assessed or planned. The present title (No 4 in the series) is the outcome of the work of a team of HM Inspectors led by a Staff Inspector. Nothing said is to be construed as implying Government commitment to the provision of additional resources.

All names of pupils appearing in the text are fictitious.

© Crown copyright 1977
First published 1977

ISBN 0 11 270444 1

Part I Working Party Report

1   Introduction

Ideas of 'giftedness' vary widely. The term is used to describe the manifest skills of the outstanding musician, dancer or artist. But it is also associated at other times with powerful intellect and with the less spectacular performances of the promising mathematician, poet or philosopher. Even within the same subject or field of activity, the term 'gifted' is applied to widely varying levels of achievement and performance. In school, some use the term to describe above average competence; others would reserve it solely for the display of rare brilliance.

Educational researchers too, have different ideas of giftedness. Most regard giftedness as a general attribute, akin to exceptional intelligence. Indeed these researchers often take an intelligence quotient (IQ) of 130 or higher as the base-line for their studies. Some speak of a small percentage of the 'most intelligent' of the population. Other researchers believe giftedness to be a collection of behavioural traits such as the tendency to resist authority, the display of initiative, curiosity or exceptional persistence. A few have studied specific gifts and talents.

The task and the team
Against this background of differing ideas of giftedness, a team of HM Inspectors set out in May 1975 to examine how gifted children fare in middle and in comprehensive secondary schools in England and Wales. This report describes how the team worked and what they found in respect of the ideas of giftedness, the practices of identification, and the various forms of provision. It makes recommendations and suggestions based upon this evidence.

The team consisted of 15 Inspectors from England, one from Wales and an Inspector from the Scottish Education Department who attended as an observer. The specialist skills of individual team members covered most subjects in the secondary school curriculum.

The collection of evidence
We collected evidence in three ways. We made visits, asked other HM Inspectors for information and made some use of data from the National Secondary Survey (NSS) of schools which was in progress at the time of our own survey:

Team visits. This report is based on visits by team members and other HMI to over 130 comprehensive and middle schools (see Appendix, Table 1). Half of these had previously been identified, with the help of district Inspectors, as schools likely to identify and to make provision for gifted pupils. The schools visited vary in size, type, age range and locality. In the schools, we observed lessons and other activities, studied examples of pupils' work and school records, and talked to teachers and their pupils.

The outcome of these visits is a picture of the variety of attitudes towards, and ways of providing for, gifted pupils. It is a qualitative rather than a quantitative picture of representative practice, indicating the difficulties that schools encounter as well as providing examples of good practice.

Other HM Inspectors. From district Inspectors we learned of the practices and attitudes of local education authorities. They told us of LEA policies for the gifted, listed details of provision for which LEA advisory staff took responsibility, and described the relationships of LEAs with voluntary agencies in various parts of the country.

From subject specialist Inspectors and committees we learned of the views of subject teachers on specific forms of giftedness. Together with specialists in the team they contributed to the second part of this report, which notes the signs of giftedness in a selection of subjects.

National Secondary Survey (NSS). The National Secondary Survey is an extended study by HM Inspectors of certain key aspects of secondary schools in England and Wales including English, mathematics and science. The size of the sample to be visited is 10 per cent of all schools. We were able to ask questions about gifted pupils as a part of this large and much more extensive survey. Our own team visits were independent of this exercise. The NSS will not be complete until 1979, but at the time of writing we had information from visits by NSS teams to about 100 secondary comprehensive schools, in addition to our 130. This provided a small sample of schools which helps to indicate the typical situation across the country. (See Appendix, Table 2.)

In addition to these three sources, we looked at evidence in the form of local, national and international views and practices. These views, expressed at conferences and meetings or on paper, served to alert us to issues in relation to gifted pupils. This report, however, is not a digest of views but the product of HMI findings based upon visiting.

The intention and the outcome

It was our intention to examine the differing ideas of giftedness current in schools. However, we felt that we should also have ready our own working definition of giftedness. This was to serve two purposes; to provide ourselves with an agreed statement to facilitate discussion within the inspection team, and to enable us to respond to teachers who held no clear ideas about giftedness, and who wanted some clarification of the nature of our enquiries. Accordingly, the following definition of gifted children was adopted at the outset:

'Children between 8 and 18:
who are generally recognised by their schools as being of superior all-round intellectual ability, confirmed where possible by a reliable individual intelligence test giving an IQ of 130 or more;
or
who exhibit a markedly superior developmental level of performance and achievement which has been reasonably consistent from earlier years;

or
of whom fairly confident predictions are being made as to continual rapid progress towards outstanding achievement, either in academic areas or in music, sport, dance or art; and
whose abilities are not primarily attributable to purely physical development.'

A narrow definition would have precluded us from examining the widely differing ideas of giftedness which we met. In addition we examined the variety of forms of identification of and provision for gifted children. These findings constitute Part I of the report.

We were conscious that a number of questions about provision for the gifted were matters of public debate during the course of our survey. For example, 'Should there be separate schools for the gifted?' 'Are gifted children in ethnic minority groups difficult to identify?' 'Is maladjustment common among the gifted?' Some answers to such questions may well be found embedded in the report, but the questions certainly cannot be treated in a simplistic fashion. The answers differ according to the concepts of giftedness and to the combination of local circumstances that affect the decisions that a school or LEA must make.

Finally, it was our intention to write a constructive document; one which would be helpful to the LEA, school or classroom teacher. The report is studded with examples which are, we hope, illustrative of practice in the very diverse patterns of school provision in England and Wales. Our collective views about general policy and practice are the subject of Chapter 3.

In other documents much has been written about general giftedness, or exceptional intelligence. For our part we felt that it would be constructive to include some views on specific forms of giftedness, based upon HMI's experience of visiting schools. Part II is therefore a collection of papers about giftedness in school subjects, some written by individual HMIs and some by specialist committees within the Inspectorate. They are more speculative than the collective team views of Part I and constitute a resource to be dipped into according to the interest of the reader.

Together, the two parts of the report are designed to map out what has for many people been largely unexplored territory.

What We Found

Enviromental 227 3911
Health : Rodent Control

The approach

This chapter is in four sections. First, we give a short description of the general state of comprehensive school reorganisation at the time of the survey. Second, we report upon the attitude of schools towards the notion of giftedness, showing the effect of local influences. Third, we review the procedures for identifying giftedness, and finally we indicate the types of provision which are to be found.

The middle and secondary comprehensive school setting

In broad terms, comprehensive schools are those which accept all-comers. They are schools 'where arrangements for the admission of pupils are not based on selection by reference to ability or aptitude' (Education Act 1976). The movement towards comprehensive schools varies widely in form and degree. In January 1976, among the 97 English LEAs:

In only three LEAs had all of the secondary schools been comprehensive for more than five years.

One in ten of the maintained secondary school population aged 11 and above was in a grammar (selective) school.

The problem of generalisation about comprehensive schools is compounded by the fact that their evolution is not only at different stages in different LEAs, but takes different forms. One of the major differences in form is between a two tier primary/secondary system and one in which three or more tiers are involved, such as a first, middle and upper school system.

Some generalisations about the national picture of middle schools may help to set our findings in broad context. At the time of this survey (1975–6 figures) middle schools:

span various age ranges between 8 and 13; 8–12 and 9–13 years are the most common, but ranges of 9–12, 8–13, 10–13, 11–13 and so on can be found in both three and four tier systems. The age range and the position of the school in relation to other tiers in the years of compulsory schooling has a marked effect upon the staffing and organisation of middle schools;

are geographically unevenly distributed, both in number and type. For example, the Midlands and the South show greater concentrations of 8–12 schools, while in the North, 9–13 and 10–13 schools tend to predominate;

vary in size very widely. The mean size of English middle schools is approximately 380 pupils compared with figures of 200 for primary and 880 for secondary schools. In this survey, middle schools visited by HMI varied in size from a 134 pupil 9–13 school to a 700 pupil 9–13 school. In the total range of all middle schools an even greater variation is to be found;

vary widely in internal organisation and ethos. One school may adopt a substantially undifferentiated non-specialist organisation which is virtually indistinguishable from that found in the majority of primary schools. In another, the school organisation and ethos may closely approximate to the early years of secondary schooling. Yet in others there may be neither a primary nor a secondary tradition, but an attempt to establish a special response to the rapid physical, intellectual and social development of children as they pass through the middle years of schooling.

These facts alone indicate that it can be extremely difficult to formulate generalisations about a system that is still at an early stage of evolution. During visits to schools, any local or transitional factors (such as the coexistence of grammar and newly created comprehensive schools) which might influence a school's view of giftedness had to be kept clearly in mind.

What the schools think

One set of questions we posed in the schools was about giftedness as a concept. Was giftedness a matter which the school had thought about? Did teachers wish to identify the gifted? Did it follow that the school was prepared to identify the gifted and to allocate resources for their support? Answers to these questions seemed fundamental to the enquiry. One difficulty bedevilled our consideration of attitudes which were held by the schools. Was 'giftedness' to be regarded as a set of general attributes (to be equated, perhaps, with general intelligence) or as one or more specific attributes (such as musical talent)? To some extent the teachers helped to solve the dilemma. When we asked questions of teachers as subject specialists, they tended to see giftedness as a specific attribute. When we asked questions of them as class teachers, the responses were in the more general sense. In the following section views of giftedness are expressed in this general sense.

We found at least half a dozen distinct attitudes towards the acceptance or non-acceptance of giftedness. Each view merits separate attention, although in practice we found that in some schools more than one view was held:

'We decline to . . .' Some schools had little wish to consider giftedness. In one school teachers refused to identify giftedness on the grounds that in a school which purported to be comprehensive, it was wrong to recognise a special category of pupils for whom some unusual provision might be made. The only school in which this extreme view was encountered was one where strong egalitarian views were held by the staff. Paradoxically, the staff were not averse to the recognition of a remedial category which was segregated out for special treatment, nor to the thesis that individual needs should be identified and provided for. Although outright refusal was encountered only once, strong reluctance to identify giftedness was not uncommon. Quite often this reluctance reflected preconceptions regarding the type of provision which might be made. 'We don't want a jet set here' or 'We've only just come from a selective system' suggested that the recognition of giftedness necessarily implied segregated forms of provision. In some areas where reorganisation was seen as a means of creating opportunity for pupils from a wider spectrum of social class and ability than under a selective system, teachers told us that LEAs were reluctant to make policy moves which might be construed by the local electorate as an injudicious selection of an elite.

'We are indifferent to . . .' Some schools appeared to be indifferent rather than hostile to the concept of giftedness. This apparent indifference seemed to have two possible causes. One was that a school might be so preoccupied with other priorities that it really could not generate any concern for this small minority. In 'difficult' schools, where vandalism, truancy and classroom control were matters of high concern, the discussion of giftedness might be regarded as a very low priority.

The other can be bluntly summarised in the comment made in an 11–16 comprehensive school: 'They (gifted children) can quite well look after themselves'.

Later in this chapter, the view that 'the gifted can look after themselves' is examined in the context of the provision for gifted children (or lack of it). Here it is enough to note that if the view implies that neither recognition nor provision is necessary, then it is at variance with the aspiration of those who teach in comprehensive schools to accept and cater for individual differences throughout the full ability range.

'We neglect to . . .' Most schools were neither reluctant to consider giftedness nor indifferent to the matter. The plain fact was that 'giftedness' as a concept had not been thought about. This was especially true of middle schools, although there were a few notable exceptions. In one HMI survey involving seven middle schools, which were deliberately chosen in the expectation of finding children of very high ability, the reaction typified findings elsewhere:

'Heads and assistant teachers manifested great uncertainty about what constituted giftedness and great reluctance to identify any of their pupils as possessing it. Out of more than 1300 pupils currently in the schools, only four were named by heads, and those with a certain diffidence.'

This is about 0·3 per cent of this school population. The same survey concludes:

'What emerged most clearly was that the teachers visited had thought very little, if at all, about giftedness, remained uncertain about what it was and how they should react to it.'

In some cases, teachers had begun to think about giftedness as a result of some agency or event that did not usually influence the school. Here are some examples:

i. A pilot LEA testing procedure revealed a high proportion of children with IQ scores of 140-plus.
ii. A local museum reported that young pupils were attending a

Saturday class which was geared to a high level of scientific understanding, and intended for older pupils.

iii. A school had been asked to participate in trials of the Schools Council Enrichment Project (SCCEP) material.

iv. An active branch of the National Association of Gifted Children had approached the school.

v. A member of staff had participated in a national in-service training course on exceptional children.

vi. A charitable trust was making awards to high achievers.

vii. A national project competition attracted the interest of middle school pupils.

These agencies often had the effect of 'alerting' a school to a consideration of the problems of identifying individual differences in general, and sometimes of giftedness in particular. Our own enquiries often resulted in a consideration of giftedness where formerly there had been none. In an 11–18 inner city comprehensive with a high percentage of immigrant pupils, a member of our team reported:

'Several members of staff commented upon the salutary nature of this HMI enquiry in that it had drawn the staff's attention to an area which had previously been overlooked.'

This particular school had other priorities to consider, but, having been alerted to the question of recognition of giftedness, began to define and to note various expressions of giftedness.

A second aspect of neglect was due not to preoccupation with other matters, but to a frank admission of inability to define and recognise giftedness. Some heads had made efforts to establish criteria, but found it virtually impossible to use anything but the most subjective measures (see the following section on Identification).

'We are obliged to . . .' Schools which serve communities with high expectations for their children may be expected to recognise giftedness. Such areas include those serving middle class 'commuter-belt' communities. There may be other pressures of parental expectation. For example, in a large comprehensive school with 20 per cent immigrant children we were told:

'Teaching is held in high esteem among the ethnic minority communities and the gifted are supported in their efforts by their families, who, with the example of the teachers before their eyes, realise that they are not necessarily condemned to the more menial, unskilled occupations.'

The second direction from which 'forced pressure' comes is from the children themselves. While some gifted children can quietly and unobtrusively accept teaching method and content which is inappropriate for them, others sometimes force schools to become aware of their giftedness through maladjusted or disruptive behaviour. This may lead to referral to an educational psychologist who, as a part of routine diagnosis, finds high general mental ability. Some pupils 'force' a system to recognise them in other ways. For example, of a 12-year-old at a comprehensive high school a head reported:

'It is impossible to insist on specific tasks for one child who refused to hand anything in on 'monsters' except a blank sheet because he said monsters were whatever one was afraid of internally and their variety was impossible to count, list or describe. Eventually he did write a piece when the teacher, contrary to his expectations, encouraged him to think in abstract terms. He does not always see 'the value of evidence' if he has worked out and 'answered' a problem or issue for himself. He is quick to reveal impatience or distaste when a particular stimulus provided by the teacher does not turn him on at all.'

A school may become alerted to the presence or arrival of a gifted pupil by comment from primary school, parents, or other factors outside the school. In one school we were told:

'A high IQ pupil due to enter the school in September 1976 has already been identified through a special letter from the feeder school and a visit by the parents. The boy has an IQ of 150, is said to be dyslexic and has been a disruptive influence in primary classes because of his eagerness to answer all questions and not to allow the others the chance.'

It cannot be said that such children have the effect of changing policy within a school. It is rare that the presence of one 'awkward' gifted child will lead a school to a broader consideration of the problems of recognition and provision.

'We are required to . . .' In contrast to those LEAs which, some teachers claim, avoid consideration of giftedness on the grounds that it is injudicious (see 'We decline to . .,'), in a few localities, it was the LEAs which asked schools to alert them to cases of pupils who might:

require enrichment programmes (four LEAs);

transfer early from primary to secondary education (two LEAs);

transfer to independent schools (one LEA).*

There is little evidence that LEAs have a quantitative measure, a set of criteria or a definition of giftedness which accompanies these requests. At the time of writing, one LEA supplied a checklist of attitude characteristics (which was compiled by university researchers), another LEA was deploying advisory staff to assist with identification, and a third had plans for utilising batteries of tests to screen for high IQ.

The effect of asking an LEA officer if there was a policy on giftedness was sometimes that a review of identification or provision was instigated. Therefore it is possible that more LEAs are now asking schools for information. Ten out of seventy LEAs indicated that

* The Secretary of State is no longer prepared to approve arrangements for the take up by LEAs of places at independent schools where this involves selection by ability or aptitude except in relation to ability or aptitude in music, including singing or dancing.

they were going to instigate a review, designate a responsible officer, or set up a working party on giftedness, although this may not necessarily result in requests or directives to schools.

'We are accustomed to . . .' Since many schools are in a transitional state from a selective to a comprehensive school, it might be assumed that some new comprehensive schools contain former grammar school teachers who are accustomed to looking for giftedness. We do not have enough evidence to confirm or refute this assumption. The transitional state can be a period of considerable adjustment for teachers from selective schools, as the following comment from a working party member indicates:

> 'This school was created by the amalgamation of two single-sex grammar schools and a non-selective school. The energies of the school during the last two years have been devoted to the problems of becoming coeducational and comprehensive, and dealing with the kinds of problem which the grammar school staffs had not previously met. The school has developed a "sanctuary unit" for disturbed pupils. This is said to be successful. The headmaster and his staff are now returning to a closer consideration of the very able pupils to ensure that their needs are not forgotten.'

Elsewhere we found former secondary modern schools which were anxious to learn how to become aware of the very able, since their comprehensive nature was seen to free them from the low ceiling of aspiration which sometimes marked the non-selective school. The school may make this readjustment faster than its surrounding community. For example, in one rural area where the local community set little store by academic achievement, the headmaster was asked in surprise by a school governor, 'You mean to say that you will be sending some of *these* children to university?'

'We do . . .' Description of this category is intended as a preface to the next section which deals with practices of identification and provision.

We looked at claims by schools that they did recognise giftedness. They fell into three broad types. First were those that said that they did, but as far as could be ascertained did not. In one school, a visit was prompted by the head's claim to parents that 'the needs of the gifted are recognised and provided for'. We felt that such a claim would be substantiated by some criteria of giftedness, some system of noting the presence of a gifted child, or by some evidence of differentiated teaching method, content or pace. These were not observed during the visit.

The second broad category consisted of schools which regard giftedness simply as one example of individual differences for which provision might be made. Often such schools could produce evidence of sound identification, recording and provision procedures across the whole ability range. We return to these practices later in the chapter.

The third category of schools deliberately chose groups of pupils for segregated forms of provision.

**Section summary
and comment**

Perhaps the best way to summarise the attitude to the concept of giftedness which we found during the survey is to contrast the term with other categories of exceptional child such as the 'slow learner', the 'backward' or the 'handicapped'. Schools have thought about these categories, have some criteria for identification and ideas about forms of provision.

Giftedness, on the other hand, is an ill-defined term. For the vast majority of schools and their teachers it is neither implicit nor explicit in the day-to-day dialogue of school life. If there are 'gifted children' they may create problems for the school, but usually this is as *individuals*. 'Slow learners', in contrast, are provided for as a problem group. Whereas gifted children can work below their potential from lack of challenge or from personal choice, and pass unnoticed, slow learners can less easily disguise their inability to work at the level and pace of their fellows.

Two groups of schools (or more precisely, sets of teachers) do accept the notion of giftedness. Some accept the concept in an implicit way through a concern to identify and provide for *individual* differences. Others accept in an explicit way, seeing gifted children as an identifiable category which needs *group* provision. In the next sections we describe the practices of these two sets of teachers with respect to identification and provision for the gifted.

Finding the gifted

A point that is constantly reiterated throughout this report is that many schools either have not thought about giftedness or hold very imprecise notions regarding its nature, so that to suggest that school policies exist for identifying giftedness is to overstate the case.

Many schools, however, do have practices for identifying individual differences and it is worth examining those practices as they might apply to the gifted. The three most important questions in relation to identification of individual differences are, 'How are differences identified?', 'When are differences identified?' and 'How is information recorded and transmitted?'. These three questions may be related to each of the following:

Contributory school records.
Testing programmes.
Other school based assessment.
Systematic screening procedures.

Contributory school records. When pupils leave one tier of the educational system for another, to what use are the records of the lower tier or contributory school put? Primary school records are used by receiving secondary schools principally as an aid to fitting children into an existing system of school organisation. Typical uses are to group children in broad bands or sets in a secondary school, or to establish parallel classes of mixed ability. Contributory school records may contain clues to giftedness in details of high achievement, notes of deep interests or extra-curricular activity, or references to standardised tests.

In one school, members of the working party were able to compare 'giftedness' which had been identified by outstanding performance in the secondary school with primary school records. Out of six gifted children, only one had been identified as in any way outstanding in the contributory primary school. Yet, conversely, primary schools in the same area complain that 'their gifted' are not recognised at secondary school level. For example, one working party member reported:

'One primary school identifies gifted pupils as children with an IQ in excess of 140. The head claims to have had six gifted children in about six years; but (assuming some or all have transferred) there was no clear evidence of these children being or having been regarded as gifted in the high school.'

It is accepted that the data itself can present the receiving school with difficulties. For example, the practical difficulties of standardising or of interpreting records from several primary schools are considerable. Often the grades given for attainments are based upon criteria which are known only to the contributory school. Sometimes for example IQ or VR scores are quoted without details of the actual test used or without assurance that it was administered under standard conditions.

We found examples of good practice where teachers in a receiving school made visits to the contributory schools. One receiving school had carefully monitored the records received from its contributory schools over several years and knew how to interpret the data which were passed on.

When a very large number of primary schools contribute to one secondary school, this difficulty of passing on and interpreting records is compounded. The most extreme case which we encountered was one in which 40 primary schools contributed to a secondary school. The information received was so varied that very little of it could be used by the secondary school.

We found similar weaknesses in the transmission and use of records between middle schools and upper schools. In three LEAs the system of transfer from middle to upper school had been examined by HMI in previous surveys. Here is a typical quotation:

'Records made by the contributory middle school are full. They include IQ (more than one administration, with name of test), and good extended comment by staff but they are not fully used by the upper school staff who tend to rely on their own observations.'

With the exception of musical or sporting achievement, which is usually made known to a receiving school, specific ability fares no better. Indications of deep interests or exceptional achievement are not often noted, or transmitted. A working party member reported the following example from an LEA where transfer took place from a middle to upper secondary school at 13-plus:

'A fourth form boy provides an interesting case. At his middle school, he had reached a high level in an individual maths learning system and had virtually completed all the prepared material. When he was transferred to the upper school, he said that he needed more difficult work, but the mathematics department said they had doubts about his real ability and suspected that he had perhaps rushed and not fully understood the work which he had done at his middle school. Such an occurrence is not uncommon, according to the head of the mathematics department. The parents of the boy then intervened and further investigation proved that the boy was in fact particularly able.'

There is, in our view, a notable lack of cross checking between the contributory and receiving school records to see if high specific or general achievement in one school is paralleled with that in the other. This shortcoming may occur once in a primary/secondary system, twice in a first/middle/upper school system and more frequently if a child changes school for other reasons.

Testing programmes. This sub-section deals with the use of standardised tests at, or immediately after, the point of pupil entry into the middle and comprehensive schools. We found that:

Most secondary schools use standardised tests of general ability (intelligence tests) only in the first year. The main purpose is to fit children into the existing school organisation.
Some schools, as a matter of policy, do not test at all. For example in a 13-plus upper comprehensive we were told: 'It has been a policy of the school since its inception to avoid the use of IQ tests. This policy has been due to a desire not to create self fulfilling predictions and to avoid the early categorisation of pupils.'
Most teachers admit that they have insufficient knowledge of the available standardised tests, the purposes for which they may be used and the limitations on their value. 'IQ' headings in school records rarely indicated whether they were individual or group tests, raw scores or standardised scores (a point previously noted in contributory school records).
Some teachers point out that the forms of giftedness which interest them are specific, and do not lend themselves to standardised testing (see Part II).
One in six schools which try to identify general giftedness uses IQ tests (NSS figures).

This is an appropriate point to make reference to LEA testing practices and also to digress somewhat from the structure of the chapter to discuss maladjustment.
In some LEAs, there is a reluctance to test at all. Often this stems from the use, in the past, of testing as a device for selection, rather than for diagnosis. Diagnostic testing takes place on a small scale when LEA educational psychologists administer tests to individual pupils who are referred to them for various reasons. The administration and interpretation of such tests are likely to have considerably more significance than school administered group tests. For this reason, high scores found by educational psychologists are sometimes useful in the identification of giftedness.
During the collection of evidence for this report, there was in the

press and on television some discussion of the gifted, which suggested an association between maladjustment and general giftedness. The matter seems to us to need more detailed examination than we could give with the time and resources available. We met few children who were said by their teachers to be both gifted and maladjusted, for cases of severe maladjustment are in special schools (including some for the gifted maladjusted) which we did not visit, these being outside our remit. Disturbed children were referred to in several schools and in our view such cases were divided between children who were maladjusted, and happened to be gifted as well, and those who suffered distress as the result of having to conform to the pressures of inappropriate teaching method, content, or the lower aspirations of less gifted classmates. Of the examples we encountered, schools had generally taken action to alleviate the cause of maladjustment by appropriate provision.

In ideal circumstances, the work of educational psychologists who are able to diagnose high general ability would clearly help to discover signs of hidden potential. For example, we heard of two children with serious reading difficulties who were found by LEA psychologists to be highly intelligent. Expert testing would probably help to reveal those gifted pupils with linguistic or cultural handicaps, such as the immigrant pupil newly arrived in this culture, or the socially deprived indigenous pupil. Individual testing by trained psychologists is costly and time consuming and it is not surprising that LEAs feel unable to test in this way on a wide scale. We know of one LEA which planned to screen all pupils for very high general ability, and of another which was testing part of the school population to assist a research project.

Other school based assessment. Since identification of gifted children owes little to school or LEA testing it is the teacher who is in the front line when it comes to identification. Inevitably, good 'giftedness spotting' is dependent upon the presence of someone who can spot, and who is not too busy to do it. If a teacher is preoccupied with other priorities, or has little sensitivity to signs of giftedness, a child may pass unnoticed. The general picture is exemplified by the comment of a member of our working party: 'There is no overall policy for identification. Identification is a hit and miss affair, the initiative coming mainly from individual teachers'.

We noted that as far as specific giftedness was concerned, teachers were often highly skilled in noting signs of outstanding potential, as well as actual performance, and there is reason to suppose that for many curricular areas such teachers are the most effective as well as the most immediate agent for identification. We were able to elicit views of what constituted giftedness in specific areas, and some of the criteria provided by teachers are incorporated into Part II of this report.

On the other hand, teachers vary widely in their qualification to teach a particular subject and in their sensitivity to children. Subject specialists in our working party saw schools in which some teachers were not specialists in the subject or curricular area which they were teaching. We have no reason to conclude that high qualifications or their equivalent in performance are an essential prerequisite to a teacher's ability to identify giftedness. We met teachers who, although highly qualified, were insensitive to the actual or potential presence of gifted children. We are not so much concerned with the fact that schools have 'spotters' of varying skill: that is inevitable. What we are concerned about is that skill in identification is utilised in a chance manner, and that some children are overlooked. This is not necessarily inevitable.

Systematic screening procedures. The various shortcomings of identification procedures suggest the need for more systematic ways of looking for extremes of individual ability, in the context of identification of individual differences. We pointed out at the beginning of this section that it would be an overstatement to say that we found a complete model for identifying giftedness. However, elements of a systematic screening policy lie in some of the following examples noted by working party members:

i. Pastoral care:
  'Particular giftedness is identified by any member of staff. The head is particularly anxious to increase the sensitivity of all adults, including parents, towards the strengths of the pupils, and time for frequent discussion and liaison increases this awareness. Great emphasis is placed upon the dissemination of information from these discussions to the house tutors who meet weekly. It is at this time that particular performance is monitored together with recognition of "giftedness" within the school.'
  (11–18 comprehensive, 650 pupils.)
ii. Periodic evaluation to note possible underachievements:
  'Lately a system of periodic assessment has been adopted that allows for a review of pupils' progress across the curriculum. One of the intentions of this review is to help staff note a pupil's achievements in one area and to question whether these match his achievements in another. Senior staff, including the headmaster, agreed that such procedures do not necessarily identify those pupils who are underachieving. The deputy headmaster suggested that there was a need in school to develop "indicators of unusual intelligence". Such indicators, he suggested, might be revealed in such activities as quiz contests, individual topic work, discussions with a teacher, choice of reading. Once the exceptional was noticed, he saw a need for pupils to be given a number of standardised tests, including one of intelligence.'
  (14–18 comprehensive, 1800 pupils.)
iii. Review of work at the point of upward movement to sixth form provision, or some higher tier:
  'Within the upper school each subject teacher awards a grade on a ten point scale at half termly intervals, and the profile for each pupil is reviewed by his senior tutor, a member of staff with pastoral responsibility for approximately 350 pupils in years 4 and 5. While this is a general monitoring exercise, a deliberate check is kept on the progress of able pupils and their teachers are encouraged to provide them with additional reading. At sixth form level, each pupil has regular interviews with his "supervisor"

who is provided with grades for effort and achievement in each subject studied.'

(11–18 comprehensive, 1750 pupils.)

Section summary and comment

The dominant means of identifying specific forms of giftedness is random and subjective teacher impression. It is random because some teachers are so preoccupied in coping with the multifarious activities of a busy class that the diagnosis of giftedness will have none of the privacy and concentration that, say, a doctor will have in considering the health of a patient.

It is random because some teachers, while accepting that there will be children with gifts, may be uncertain of their manifestation. For example, a non-specialist who is teaching English (and there are many) is unlikely to have the insights of his specialist colleague.

It is random because provision for some school activities may require unusual physical plant, hardware, extended time, or other factors. In some subjects there must be provision before identification can take place. This is especially true of some physical activities, of music and of art.

A related difficulty is that for some activities, for example sport and music, time lost before identification is claimed to be time that can never be regained. It is no use for a girl to be identified as a gifted gymnast in the last year of school. She needs to be identified much earlier within the school or elsewhere. This is part of the more general difficulty of timing the identification of giftedness.

It is subjective because few satisfactory measures of a more objective nature exist for specific forms of giftedness. It is conceivable that test batteries might be compiled to indicate potential giftedness as a complement to subjective judgement, but at the moment this is a very rare form of identification. Good subjective judgement, by expert judges, is more appropriate for several areas of the curriculum than inappropriate attempts at using objective tests.

It is also subjective because teachers in specialist areas rarely reduce idiosyncrasies by working as a team to pool their concepts of giftedness and their perceptions of it in a particular child, or to agree in any quantitative way who shall or shall not count as gifted.

Attempts to identify general giftedness are based upon the records of contributory schools and tests administered in school. In our view, although we have serious reservations about the effectiveness of the existing practice of collection and transmission of data from school to school, such material can provide clues to underachievement.

There will remain those children who will miss being identified for lack of opportunity, through the inconsistent nature of identification, or through any of the other factors we have mentioned.

We noticed that it was possible to visit schools where no gifted child had ever been identified, and this could not simply be accounted for by the fact that the schools had other priorities or were in some way opposed to identification. The NSS sample showed that half the comprehensive schools had identified pupils with 'superior intellectual ability' or specific gifts (see Appendix, Table 2, for details).

How do schools provide for the gifted?

Once a school has recognised that it has gifted children, a decision has to be made about the most appropriate provision for their support. The decision is an *ad hoc* matter in the vast majority of schools, rather than one of school or LEA policy. The bases for the decision are conditioned by such factors as the school's view of giftedness (specific or general), the school's assessment of its capacity to provide and the number of pupils involved. To take extreme cases, one school may decide that provision can best be made by agencies outside the school, while another may be confident that it has adequate resources for the support of the gifted without enlisting any outside aid. For the majority of schools, provision for the gifted lies between these extremes, but for convenience of presentation we consider first the various forms of 'out-of-school' provision and then forms of 'in-school' provision.

Out-of-school provision

Transfer. The most extreme form of provision is to transfer a pupil to another school. The school might be in the same tier, or it might be at a higher level.

Transfer to a school within the same tier occurs when the receiving school is seen to have special facilities which the identifying school does not possess. For example, a gifted musician is thought to require additional specialist teaching: the LEA may have a school which has a particularly well-endowed department which can teach to a high level. Such 'outward' transfer is very rare in the middle and lower secondary schools, but not unknown at sixth form level.

It is a practice which is possible in areas where schools are closely grouped and where there are complementary strengths in sixth form teaching. One school may have well-developed engineering science provision while a neighbouring school may have strong biology provision. These conditions are likely to obtain in urban communities, but while schools elsewhere may have considered such arrangements, the practice is rare, mainly for logistical reasons. For example a working party member reported:

'Transfer has been made available at the sixth form level, but the situation of the school in the south of the county makes travel expensive and difficult. The nearest centres are in a neighbouring authority and across-county payment creates barriers.'

Transfer may also involve crossing the LEA/independent school boundaries, which may cause difficulty or embarrassment to an LEA. For example, a gifted musician who could not be catered for in a small (650) 11–18 comprehensive school applied to a local independent school which is well-known for good music provision. There was some political objection to LEA support.

Transfer 'outward' for children of very high general ability rarely occurs in areas which are fully comprehensive. However, one LEA utilised places in the independent sector to 'cater for the needs of children who are exceptionally gifted'. The LEA saw this as an intermediate step towards catering for the needs of the gifted within the maintained system.

The opinions of teachers regarding the desirability of transfer 'outward' were varied. Several heads were adamant in their view that gifted children should be transferred and educated in local, regional or national centres. Conversely there was an equally strong body of opinion which is typified in the remark of a head of department:

> 'These gifts (general giftedness) do not necessitate removal from a normal (comprehensive secondary) school provided that the normal school is staffed and organised to cater for a "full ability range".'

Transfer 'upward' takes place when a child moves from one tier to the next at an earlier age than usual. For example, a pupil might miss the final year of his primary school to enter the first year of secondary school. The practice is based upon the assumption that the child has a markedly superior development and achievement to those of his contemporaries. While common sense suggests that there will be children who will be several years in advance of their fellows in some respects, the difficulty of making a decision to move pupils 'upward' is increased by not knowing if the child is ready in all respects. We heard of instances where early transfer had resulted in anxiety, unhappiness or failure for the child. LEAs are usually sensitive to these dangers and either refuse to allow early transfer or do their best to limit early transfer to situations where there is:

> total agreement by pupil, parent and both heads;
> screening by LEA educational psychologists, using appropriate tests and including an individual intelligence test; and
> strong indication that the pupil possesses a broad spectrum of giftedness and is not likely to suffer from being in a more adult social environment.

The cases of early transfer which we met were between primary and secondary schools. It was not met between first and middle schools, or between middle and upper schools. The practice of 'promotion' of a child (which is dealt with later) sometimes leads to early transfer from the secondary to the tertiary level.

Partial transfer. A less extreme form of transfer is 'partial' transfer, where a pupil spends some part of the school week in another institution, while remaining in the original school for most purposes. At the middle school level we encountered only one example. This was the attachment of a group of particularly able 13-year-old mathematicians to a class in a nearby FE college. At secondary school level the practice varied. It was not uncommon where as a matter of expediency and staff utilisation two comprehensive schools provided one high level course on one campus. Two single-sex comprehensives might agree to rationalise their provision in this way.

In a few areas, initiatives have been taken as part of a broader policy of looking at 16-plus provision in a locality. For example we noted that:

> 'The school coordinates its timetable with the local technical college and with the centre for advanced studies to enable pupils

in the sixth and seventh years to join their courses too if wished.'
(11–18 comprehensive, 2200 pupils.)

In another school, an interesting course leading to the International Baccalaureate was planned and operated in conjunction with the local college of further education.

These examples were not organised specifically with gifted children in mind, but the practice of partial transfer does seem to offer opportunities to gifted children without the dangers and difficulties of complete transfer. One problem of any institutional cooperation of this kind lies in harmonisation of timetables.

LEA provision. A local education authority can provide 'outside' support for gifted pupils in several ways. It can, for example, make grants, run courses for pupils, establish special centres for music, sport or languages, provide peripatetic teachers, or offer in-service courses to teachers in the schools.

Grants to individual children are the most overt form of support. They can be for the purpose of transfer or partial transfer to private institutions or can be for the purchase of special tuition or equipment. Such schemes are not always popular with LEAs. They require selection and therefore some fairly elaborate screening procedure. They require the attention of LEA officers to be directed towards particular individuals, whereas the sheer size of local authorities necessitates preoccupation with group provision. Despite these difficulties, LEAs do support gifted performers in music and sport. Grants to children who are more generally gifted are unlikely to be found. We know of three LEAs which give grants or make premises available to the National Association for Gifted Children (NAGC) for the support of Saturday classes. The activities of NAGC, though intended to challenge and to provide opportunities for gifted children, are nevertheless available to all-comers and there is no selection test.

Provision which is intended for the full ability range and which is in theory available to all children can be of especial help to the gifted. For example, one LEA pays local artists to demonstrate, lecture or give short courses to schools. Several LEAs run Saturday art classes. Such arrangements may extend the chances of a child with artistic gifts to acquire insights into art which are different from those normally developed by the school.

In most LEAs, various forms of central resource are available to schools and to individual pupils. There may be a music, physical education, craft, field studies or language centre available, together with special staff. There is every reason to believe that the gifted children who have access to these resources put them to good use. There is a neutrality about LEA central resources that makes schools more willing to use them than they would be to use the resources of a nearby school. In addition, many of the central resources are utilised out of school time so that organisational problems are minimal. LEA central provision supports specific forms of giftedness and schools are usually happy to transfer this responsibility. For example a working party member reported:

'The head considered that once the school had passed a pupil gifted in music or physical activities to the County organisation "It is the County's job". The LEA does have numerous orchestras, coaching facilities . . .'
(11–16 comprehensive, 1100 pupils.)

We heard of two cases where an LEA ran short courses for gifted mathematicians outside school time.

LEA centres involve the movement of children on a large scale. An alternative is for an LEA to employ specialist peripatetic teachers who move into schools. Again, the intention is often to provide support for a subject or curriculum area, rather than for the needs of an individual pupil, but in practice the child with specific gifts will get a good deal of individual attention if his/her ability is in a performance area such as music, sport, art or drama. Schools look upon peripatetic teachers as one valuable arm of support for specific giftedness and fear the diminution of support as economic cuts result in the cutting of peripatetic work.

We found that two LEAs had teacher advisers for gifted children. Six had an assistant education officer or general adviser with responsibility for the gifted as a part of other tasks, and ten had committees or working parties looking at 'the problem of giftedness'.

Local expertise. Some schools were alert to the possibility of using local experts to support gifted individuals. Local experts might be retired people with special interests, hobbies or skills, or they might be professional lecturers with flexible working hours. There were few reports of such help, for we are now speaking of voluntary help, and not individuals contracted by an LEA. Sometimes the support was sporadic. For example a university lecturer was in the habit of 'dropping in' to help gifted scientists whenever he could spare the time. In these cases there was no way in which the working party could gauge the nature of the interaction.

Teachers did not resent the introduction of local expertise, for often it was they who had invited the expert into the school. A few schools had organised systems of using local expertise informally. For example, some secondary schools had made contact with local industry and knew that they could obtain expert help or advice for gifted children at work on advanced technological projects. We visited a middle school where the head had established a register of retired or available local experts who were willing to help groups or individuals.

Parents. Teachers were convinced that the most significant form of outside help which a school, or rather a pupil, receives was that of parental interest and encouragement. Perhaps the experience of one school is sufficient to illustrate the point:

'All pupils mentioned how very dependent they were on parental support and interest and one girl gymnast suggested that she would not have persevered in her training had it not been for her family's interest and sharing in her successes. Examples were cited of other gifted boys and girls who had given up because parental

support was not forthcoming'—and from the point of view of teachers at the same school: 'Success in this activity, teachers suggest, is very dependent on strong parental support and encouragement and this is cultivated with plenty of opportunities provided for parental involvement and consultation.'
(14–18 comprehensive.)

Two points of interest emerge from this quotation (and other examples which we met). First, in some areas, the anxiety of parents for their children to excel needs no encouragement, and indeed can sometimes put too great a strain on pupils.

The second point is that if the emergence of giftedness depends to a large degree upon home conditions, schools may have to decide to make compensatory provision where parental support is lacking for whatever reason. For example, in one school serving an area of social deprivation, all the additional resources (teaching staff and high capitation grant) were directed into a remedial department in which one-quarter of the school received its entire curricular diet. The work of this department is unquestionably important but it might be that some school resources could have been deployed to make compensatory provision for gifted children from deprived homes. In the example mentioned above, we noted that parental support was not a spontaneous matter and that much credit for arousing parental interest could be attributed to the teachers.

In-school provision

This section is concerned with what schools attempt to do for themselves, without the help of outside support. We look first at the forms of internal organisation which, we were told, can support the specific or general forms of giftedness. Provision can be broken down into two rough categories: the effects of group organisation (setting, mixed ability grouping, vertical grouping) and of organisation which is designed to help individuals (promotion, acceleration, withdrawal, enrichment, differentiated homework).

Streaming. The assumption behind streaming is that general ability can be identified on the basis of former achievement or test scores. If one leaves aside the question of the validity of such assumptions, it is clear that streaming is a very crude form of provision for the gifted. The generally gifted require a level of work or a pace of work which is higher than that of 'top' streams. Some schools have an 'express stream' which purports to meet this need by working faster than the remaining streams. The gifted, in the sense of this report, are a minority even in such streams.

Setting. Setting is a form of grouping pupils on the basis of specific achievement, rather than the general achievement which streaming assumes. Setting is a secondary school phenomenon, although we did find that 50 per cent of middle schools visited had sets for maths. While some heads felt that there was a *prima facie* case for grouping pupils of similar ability, in most areas of the curriculum, teachers had reservations about the effectiveness of setting, as a help to the gifted. Here are some observations:

'Our head *defines* gifted children as those in the top set'. Teachers regarded this as a circular definition, lacking in clarity and hindering the school from thinking about other forms of possible provision. (11–16 comprehensive, 1300 pupils.)

The act of placing a gifted child in a top set is often no more than another way of finding him a quiet corner in which to work, for a 'set' will often work at the pace of the average pupil in that set. We observed that:

'Gifted children would find themselves following a top set course and would be expected to look after themselves. There appears to be no deliberate attempt made to give differential help.' (English in an 11–16 comprehensive.)

The comprehensive with its wide spread of ability usually means that sets are less homogeneous than those in selective schools:

'The system of setting, half-term assessments of attitudes and effort and examinations twice a year goes some way to selecting and providing for the more able pupils, but can and probably does miss some gifted children—especially those with some behaviour problems. Because the average achievement of the top sets is lower than in some selective schools, teachers claim that there is difficulty in making demands on the more able pupils.' (11–16 comprehensive, 980 pupils.)

In most schools we found that setting was no more than it claimed to be; an organisational device for grouping those of roughly similar ability. In the majority of 11–16 comprehensive schools of less than 1000 pupils, even skilful setting will mean that only three or four gifted pupils are likely to be found in a 'top set'. What is far more important than the organisational device of setting is the teaching method which is employed.

An example may serve to illustrate this point. In the history department of an upper school, two teachers were observed working with parallel top history sets. One teacher used this setting as the basis for differentiated work; he encouraged project work, group work and adopted a tutorial role. The other teacher employed didactic whole class teaching method, pitched at the average ability for the set.

The setting policy of this department obviously could help the gifted since it provided scope for further differentiation. The second teacher in this illustration is, in our view, the more typical teacher working in a setted situation. While setting may hold advantages for a school in other ways, it is not of *itself* either necessary or sufficient provision for the gifted child.

Mixed ability groups. Mixed ability grouping is a form of organisation that seems to arouse strong feelings among professional educationists and laymen alike. Most of the teachers that we talked to indicated that they were either clearly 'for' or 'against' working with mixed ability groups.

Among the several reasons that were put forward for the adoption of mixed ability grouping was the belief that teaching in such groups encourages the teacher to recognise wide differences of ability between individual pupils and to attempt to cater for their differences.

The practice of mixed ability grouping was common in the middle schools we visited and in the first year or two of secondary schools. Thereafter it gave way to setting, and grouping on the basis of choice. A few subjects such as craft and some aspects of physical education were normally taught in mixed ability groups throughout schools.

While we found instances of mixed ability grouping, we had greater difficulty in finding mixed ability teaching. In other words what we saw was mixed ability groups taught by whole class methods and gifted children unchallenged by work pitched at or around the class norm. Attempts at accommodating the extremes of ability by using worksheets in the major disciplines were often unimpressive. These too were predominantly 'lock-step' and did not allow for variations in the quality of thinking. Gifted children merely finished faster than their fellows.

In general, the advocates of mixed ability teaching were realistic about its difficulties:

'Far greater care has to be taken in the preparation, organisation of activities and evaluation of work in mixed ability teaching'.
(Teachers in an 11–16 comprehensive.)

Examples of care in preparation included the compilation of written guidelines (worksheets) and/or banks of relevant reference material, and the teaching of skills such as the use of centrally-based resources (for example as school libraries).

Some teachers thought that there was a particular need to limit the size of classes containing pupils of widely mixed ability. Classroom teachers placed this between 20–25 pupils, while in laboratory and workshop situations, where a higher degree of pupil mobility was likely, they were adamant that small groups of 10, 15 or 20 (depending upon the nature of the activity and the extent of 'spread' of ability) were essential.

There is a risk that the very able may have a smaller share of teacher time than the less able. This was a viewpoint which teachers expressed with regret, and many seemed guilty about the imbalance. Yet we observed that where gifted children were identified, the work of such children was often directed in a highly skilled and appropriate manner, despite limited time for dialogue with teachers, the two preconditions for such provision being the competence of the teacher to handle mixed ability groups and his/her insight and qualification in the area being taught.

Some curricular areas are difficult to teach to mixed ability groups. Modern languages and mathematics seemed to present particular difficulties in that skills are largely interrelated and sequential (see Part II).

Mixed ability grouping posed considerable problems for the 'average and less than average teacher', the inexperienced teacher, or one working in difficult circumstances. But with the able, well-organised teacher, unpreoccupied by other pressing priorities, the gifted often fared well. For example in an 11–14 high school, two techniques of giving differentiated work appeared to be effective:

> '*Differentiated tasks.* The example given by the head of department was that when a group is doing a topic on "People on the move", some pupils might be set the task of analysing narrative and biography of famous individuals (Gladys Aylward, Marco Polo, Mao Tse Tung), while the gifted might undertake an analysis of the more abstract ideas associated with these individuals (spread of Christianity or Communism or the motives of exploration and discovery).

> *Self-programmed projects.* Tasks are planned by the pupil and plans are then submitted to the teacher for discussion and help in structuring the project, making appointments, organising transport, planning the use of time and evaluating the end product.'

We were not concerned with a comprehensive study of the problems and purposes of mixed ability grouping, but only with its effect on supporting the gifted. We found that most of the mixed ability grouping was not accompanied by appropriate teaching method. All that can be said is that while there were some first class examples of differentiated provision for the gifted in mixed ability classes (in the form of special work, individual tuition, direction to appropriate reading and demand for high standards of work) in most schools the use of whole class teaching methods or insufficiently differentiated worksheets left the highly able unchallenged and unprovided for.

Vertical grouping. At one time it was common practice for pupils to move upward through a school in each subject on the basis of achievement, rather than on a chronological basis for all subjects. The practice is rare now in this country and we found only one secondary school where it was used as the basis for grouping. The effect is to create 'homogeneous' groups not unlike those produced by setting. The advantages to the gifted are those of acceleration in subjects where they have particular strengths (see below) but there are the same basic problems which characterise setting; the gifted represent a minority within a set and may be unchallenged unless there are further opportunities for differentiated provision.

Withdrawal. It is common practice to withdraw individuals or groups of individuals temporarily from a class to provide special tuition which is appropriate to their needs. It is a costly use of staff time and cannot easily be carried out in schools which have neither the physical space nor the available staff.

In the schools visited, children who were generally gifted were not withdrawn but the withdrawal of gifted musicians or others with specific gifts was common practice to fit in with the programme of a peripatetic teacher. We found some examples of voluntary surrender of a teacher's preparation or other non-teaching time in order to offer special tuition by withdrawal of individuals or groups of children with special gifts.

In one school, a second modern language was taught to very able children who were withdrawn from the top set of a first modern language class. This was done by an enthusiastic head of modern languages at the expense of part of his timetabled administration time (11–16 comprehensive of 1200 pupils). In the same school, the headmaster was temporarily giving up some of his administration time to teach a particularly able group of children withdrawn from a mixed ability English group. In both cases, the time volunteered was made up during non-timetabled time and after school work.

Promotion. Promotion is the movement of a pupil upward through the school to a higher age group. It is not a common practice in middle schools, partly because its logical outcome is early transfer to a higher tier institution, which is a practice not favoured by middle schools. It is a very overt form of provision which presupposes all round giftedness, and advanced physical and social development.

In the secondary school, similar considerations apply. Promotion results in early arrival at the sixth form, or early transfer at 16-plus. Here is one example of promotion. It is an extract from a letter from the head of an 11–18 comprehensive (1100 pupils) to parents of pupils in the last term of the third year:

'For some years it has been the school's practice to present suitable pupils for O-level examinations after four years. This year, it may be possible for certain pupils who have just entered their fourth year to take a range of O-levels in June 1976, and enter the lower sixth in September 1976 to commence their A-level studies —thus, effectively, "jumping" the fifth form. A minimum number of O-level passes (five or, in a few cases, four) will be required of pupils wishing to make this "jump", and they will have to possess the necessary ability and industry to enable them to benefit from this course. Children who do make this rapid progress can arrive in the upper sixth with a year "in hand", when they will have the opportunity to study and read widely for university entrance awards, or take further A-levels. Alternatively, if they have already achieved good A-levels, they may leave school at 17-plus and use the year before going on to higher education in other "broadening" activities, such as foreign travel, voluntary service, or business or work experience.'

Teachers in the school held mixed views on the effectiveness and wisdom of the practice as the following note on a heads of department meeting shows:

'Expressions of agreement with the principle of early examinations were supported by the belief that the able children needed extra stimulus and that they were not fulfilling their potential under the present chronological scheme. Doubts were expressed on the grounds that children would be too immature for sixth form work, that they would have to specialise too early, that there was no evidence that the present setting system was not working though possibly greater pressure could be applied in top sets. A number of doubts and questions about the scheme were raised, in particular the arts bias, the method of choosing candidates, the complications and pressures of lower sixth work involving three A-levels and additional O-levels, the problems of teaching within the same set able children to early examination level and moderately able children in a traditional two-year course, and the unsuitability of some courses for early examinations.'

Our own estimate of the long-term effect of the practice of promotion is derived largely from teachers' anecdotes. We heard of cases that were clearly appropriate for an individual, but heard enough instances of promotion which resulted in unhappiness, loss of motivation or even failure, to be convinced that it is a risky practice unless carried out with the greatest regard for the general maturity, and not simply the academic giftedness, of a pupil. Careful monitoring of subsequent performance following promotion is essential.

Acceleration. Acceleration, in this context, means that a pupil can take individual subjects or courses earlier than the majority of a year group. In one form, it is not unlike promotion, except that a gifted child will 'move upward' for work with a higher class for some subjects but remain with his fellows for other work. In another form, it simply means that a pupil is allowed to accelerate away upon a course that all pupils will follow sooner or later. Suppose, for example, that a school uses a highly structured course to teach modern languages. The material is sequentially ordered, and presented as programmed audio-visual material. A pupil who has some gift for language might well accelerate through the course and complete the work well ahead of others, given a modicum of the teacher's time to practise oral skills.

At middle school level, in the schools visited, we saw no courses which permitted this second form of acceleration. Their absence from middle schools and their rarity in secondary schools may be attributed to the considerable organisational difficulties which the implementation of acceleration courses involves. It is also due to a shortage of good quality learning material which might enable a pupil to work for most of the time without the immediate presence of a teacher and yet receive the feedback of progress and correction which is necessary. Gifted pupils need a course which enables them to 'bound ahead'. Thus linear courses which require step by step progressions are not always helpful to the very able. If the steps are too small, gifted pupils become frustrated by the simplicity. More flexible courses which allow the pupil to change to a faster rate or to leap ahead require considerable teacher support or sophisticated software/hardware materials.

Not all areas of the curriculum lend themselves to accelerated treatment in this way, of course. It is difficult to imagine an effective accelerated self-teaching craft and design course, for example, devised upon sequential lines.

Enrichment. Enrichment was found to be one of the imprecise and overworked terms used in discussions on giftedness. The most common practice in school was to equate the word with any kind of provision, ranging from extra-curricular activities to the use of library books. This generalised use is unfortunate, since teachers often said that they 'preferred enrichment to acceleration', without being clear what enrichment might imply.

In this report, enrichment is used to indicate a change in quality of work rather than a change in quantity. For example, if a teacher gave more work of the same type of mathematical problem to gifted pupils, this would not be enrichment. If the gifted pupils taking science were given problems which called for higher levels of abstraction, together with teaching support or book resources which would involve deeper insights than those of their less able fellows, then that would be enrichment. Enrichment materials can be as general as extensive library facilities, but usually they are in the form of curriculum development material designed to improve the quality of thinking. In this sense, only one example of enrichment material was seen. It was the Schools Council Enrichment Project trials material.

At the time of writing, no formal appraisal of the material is available. The preparation of enrichment material is difficult, for there is the inbuilt limitation that gifted children have broader and more varied insights into an activity and often these cannot be taken into consideration in a set of objectives, let alone in published material. On the other hand, there were examples of teachers who were 'enriching' a planned course by suggestions of further reading, by expecting a high order of performance or analysis, or by dialogue with pupils which utilised a vocabulary or concepts well above the level used in whole class teaching. The general impression was that teachers were trying to enrich rather than call for more work of the same level or quality. In one secondary school, a mathematics textbook had ample exercises of work, but the teacher had modified both the text and the exercises for the gifted in order to 'enrich' the content by a higher level of thinking, or more complex applications of basic theory.

It was clear that a teacher's capacity to enrich was a function of his or her insight into a curricular area. The head of department would often play a vital role in deploying teachers so as to enrich a course of study. For example, in a large 11–18 comprehensive the heads of boys and girls PE had worked hard to identify among the academic staff a number of amateur sportsmen and women who could develop qualitatively richer experiences for gifted athletes. Similarly, on an informal basis, a head of physics had enlisted the aid of teachers outside his department who could enrich the physics work with their expertise in electronics and radio communication. Effective enrichment was also a function of timing; of knowing when to suggest further reading, to ask questions, or to pose difficult problems.

Differentiated homework. We found few cases where a teacher had given homework intended to differentiate between various ability levels. The overwhelming impression was that one task was given to all pupils in a class or set. If the task was that of completing a mathematics exercise, gifted pupils simply carried it out faster. Undifferentiated homework tasks usually reflected undifferentiated classroom teaching.

Librarians and libraries. In many schools, librarians constitute a valuable source of support for gifted children, as the following example illustrates:

> 'The head considers the librarian a significant resource for academically gifted children. Especially does he think this is so in a school such as his where much of the teaching is carried out in classes of mixed ability. While he would wish to avoid the setting of pupils according to ability he would encourage the withdrawal from class to consult with the librarian and to be guided by her in a course of reading that would extend gifted pupils beyond the average level of their class within a particular topic. He also sees the need to establish better communications between the librarian and other staff that would help draw the latter's attention to those pupils who are revealing unusual gifts by their choice and depth of reading.'
> (13-plus upper school, 1100 pupils.)

We looked closely at the utilisation of libraries by gifted pupils and found a somewhat unsatisfactory picture, as the following factors illustrate:

Limited budgets meant that the maintenance of the stocks of books in most general demand was a first priority to satisfy. In some cases there were just too few books, as in the 14–18 eight form entry ex-grammar school, where it was noted 'Mathematics section consists of about ten books'.

Libraries are sometimes unavailable since the space is required for teaching. In an 11–16 comprehensive school the library was used for teaching purposes 32 out of 40 periods a week.

Larger schools may have upper school libraries which are not accessible to lower school pupils:

> 'Libraries in the lower school halls are still inadequate but an advance has been made in that they are now open during the day. The school points out that younger pupils may, by agreement, borrow books from the upper school library but this is difficult to work in practice. The upper school library has a good stock of books but the available study space is often full.'
> (11–18 comprehensive, 1800 pupils.)

This is a relatively good example. In five schools visited where split library facilities exist, four upper libraries are 'out-of-bounds' to younger pupils. Despite these factors, it was noted that a number of specialist teachers and librarians were adroit in directing pupils to reading which was appropriate, and obtaining books on loan which the school could not afford to stock.

Lack of private study space. Few schools had quiet rooms or study carrels, either in libraries or in departments.

Access to equipment and other physical resources. Some forms of giftedness require access to hardware for their support and expression. Musicians require instruments, scientists require laboratory facilities, craftsmen require workshop equipment, and mathematicians may require access to computer terminals.

A school faces several difficulties in making such resources available to gifted pupils. First, the equipment may be in short supply. Second, it may be located in a place which is used for other purposes (a piano may be in a hall used for PE). Third, it may be available at certain periods only (computer terminals). Fourth, it may be potentially hazardous to use without teacher supervision. Thus it is possible that a school has a workshop available which is not timetabled for use by a class, but which cannot be used by a gifted pupil since supervisory staff are not available.

There are few solutions to these problems. Usually, teachers who hold responsibility for hardware allow pupils to use facilities under supervision in non-timetabled time. Sometimes a teacher will volunteer part of his non-teaching time in order to allow a pupil to use special equipment.

The curriculum and extra-curricular provision

The majority of schools express the view that a pupil with general gifts should follow the same curriculum as other pupils. The rationale is that the gifted pupil, like any other pupil, is at school to experience a balanced curriculum. In practice, this occurs at middle and lower secondary school level, but when options are being chosen later in secondary schooling, then the curriculum tends to narrow to exclude 'performance' subjects. Bitter complaints were voiced by some heads of departments that their most able artists, technologists, craftsmen, musicians or dramatic performers were 'lured away to academically respectable areas of the curriculum'. Sometimes there was an expansion of curriculum. For example, the generally gifted might take a second modern language, begin a classical language, or an additional science subject. In these cases, in the secondary schools visited, complaints from art, music and craft specialists still held true; the generally gifted did not come their way. On the other hand, in the schools we visited, specific giftedness was rarely found to be indulged at the expense of a balanced curricular diet. If a gifted musician had to be withdrawn from a class in order to work with a peripatetic specialist, the loss of time from that class was usually made up during extra-curricular time.

One 11–18 comprehensive school (1750 pupils) visited by members of the working party had avoided narrowing the range of required subjects which characterises so many schools in the fourth and fifth year by requiring all pupils to study English, mathematics and one subject from each of the following groups; modern languages, humanities, creative arts, sciences and 'rag bag'. The latter group consisted of a mixture of subjects so that it was possible for a pupil to take a second language or additional science subject, but not more. This pattern provides all pupils, including the gifted, with a broad and balanced curriculum up to the age of 16.

Gifted pupils are expected to take those examinations which will give entry to higher education. The General Certificate of Education examinations at Advanced Level do not always afford opportunities for gifted pupils to demonstrate the types of characteristic which are given in Part II of this document. We spoke to gifted pupils who were critical of the weight of factual information that they were expected to absorb for A-level examinations. There were complaints by them, substantiated by teachers and librarians, that some A-level syllabuses constricted the range of reading.

It is extra curricular time which gives a very useful measure of flexibility to the content, range and depth of experience which a school can offer to gifted children. We were impressed by the range of activities which teachers offered during lunch hours and after school. The advantages to all children and not simply to the gifted are considerable. Some in the list below have already been mentioned:

access to hardware resources which are not available during timetabled time;
opportunity to meet with pupils of 'like mind' and interest;
opportunity to encounter an adult with particular expertise in a hobby, study or other activity;
opportunity to select and to practise those things which a school cannot fit into its normal timetable.

These advantages are more to be found in the British educational scene than in many others and parents and pupils ought to be properly appreciative of the amount of time and energy which teachers devote to extra-curricular activity.

Type and size of school

At the beginning of this chapter, we attempted to indicate the extent of reorganisation, at the time of writing, and to warn against the danger of generalised statements concerning size and type of comprehensive school. As the body of the chapter shows, the vital factors with respect to identification and provision are not necessarily dependent upon the age range or size of school. Instead they are heavily dependent upon the awareness of individual differences which a teacher may possess, and the degree to which he or she may be prepared to learn what varieties of provision are desirable and available for an individual child.

Nevertheless, questions of size and type of school obviously affect internal organisation and consequent provision, and it is appropriate to conclude the chapter by stating what heads or teachers felt about the effects of these factors upon identification and provision.

First, the working party gained the impression that three tier systems in some cases found it more difficult to provide for the gifted than two tier systems:

i. Transfer from one school to another seems to be accompanied by some loss of documentary information on a pupil's attainment, disposition and capability. This problem was discussed under 'awareness', at the beginning of this chapter. Apart from documentary information, unwritten knowledge of pupils has to be built up from scratch at each change of school.

ii. Transfer from one school to another seems to involve some loss of 'academic momentum'. The early years in the new school are characterised by attempts to build sound foundations for work later in the school. The emphasis is upon 'common' knowledge, well learned. For the gifted, this is mastered readily; thereafter they may coast unnoticed, or become bored, and unchallenged.

iii. Transfer from one school to another means that 'senior' pupils revert to a 'junior' role in the receiving school and may be expected to display less responsibility or initiative.

iv. There may be an understandable reluctance on the part of the school to categorise pupils too early. Mixed ability groups are frequently found in the early years of a receiving school, not from any conviction that mixed ability groups are the best means of providing social integration, or of making provision for individual needs, but simply because such an organisation avoids early categorisation based upon inadequate information. The effect is exaggerated by the coupling of mixed ability organisation with the teaching of 'foundation knowledge' based upon a tightly structured course, or set of worksheets. This was a matter of some concern to the head of a receiving school:

'The headteacher suggested that 13-plus transfer and the school's consequent reluctance to categorise its first year might hold up identification—an 11-18 school on the look out for gifted pupils would undoubtedly detect them earlier. Mixed ability organisation and its 'gravitation to the mean' could mean—though this is only surmise—that, for example, the worksheet pattern of working could impede the stretching of the very able.'
(13-plus school, 1700 pupils.)

In addition to these general problems of three tier systems, those which involve a separate middle school may have special problems. For example, a child aged 8 years with all-round intellectual gifts may, if he is in an 8–12 middle school, be capable of the work beyond that of an average 11-year-old in an 11–16 comprehensive. Yet his 8–12 middle school may have much of the ethos of a primary school. It will be 'deemed primary' by DES classification and this may be reflected in the fact that the LEA may allocate the school allowances for capitation and development which are on a 'primary scale'. Staff with curricular specialisms are not likely to be in such schools.

In an LEA with 13 8–12 middle schools, of 185 teachers, 15 were trained graduates. Posts of responsibility for liaison between schools were rare. No school gave a senior post for geography, history or social studies. Heads commonly spoke of the difficulties they met in recruiting and retaining senior and specialist staff when the highest post of responsibility they could offer was scale 2. (Secondary schools may offer scale 4 or 5.)

Although this example cannot typify a complex national pattern, it is difficult to avoid the conclusion that middle schools of other age ranges and similar size would have difficulty in attracting and holding staff who in an 11–16 or 11–18 comprehensive would be making specialist knowledge and insights available to gifted children over the age of 11 years. This conclusion does not imply criticism of other aspects of work in middle schools, nor suggest that for the vast majority of children provision is ineffectual. Such implications cannot be drawn from our limited findings. We simply ask 'If highly qualified staff are not in middle schools, and if schools do not often transfer gifted pupils upward (see section on transfer) do such schools recognise gifted children and make other forms of differentiated provision?' In the schools we visited, there were good (but not well recorded) pastoral care and good extra-curricular activities. Parent/school contacts were frequent and well-informed. In-school provision was less evident than in the secondary schools. But the most important fact was that, as the section on awareness shows, middle school teachers had not often considered giftedness.

We find it very difficult to draw any definite relationship between size of comprehensive school and provision for the gifted. As we found in middle schools, a small comprehensive school (500 pupils) will have difficulties in attracting a full range of well-qualified and experienced staff, and it will need to look to out-of-school provision to support its handful of gifted pupils. There may be a temptation to assume that a large (1500 pupils) 11–18 comprehensive will have better material resources, a greater range of graded posts, and greater opportunity for flexibility. In some cases we found this to hold true, but in others there are disadvantages; a big school may have split site working; poor teaching may be hidden in a large department; a school catchment area may be one of social deprivation; a head may lack the managerial skills which such a large institution requires; a large remedial group may present major problems which outweigh the individual problems of the gifted, and so on. The size of the school, along with other factors such as local staying-on rates and other provision for 16-plus education, becomes more significant in considering the provision for the older gifted pupil. In the schools visited, some sixth forms were too small and self-contained and unable to provide for the gifted. This is not to say that the school may not contain individual teachers of high calibre in some subjects.

We derived the firm impression that too many of the small schools visited could not provide range or depth or special advice on career choice beyond a vague expectation of moving gifted pupils on to higher education. Very few schools had developed cooperative sixth form work with nearby institutions or looked to other forms of outside provision.

3   Conclusions and Suggestions

Awareness

What can a school do if it wishes to become more aware of gifted children? In the body of this report we drew attention to the range of definitions of giftedness and to the diverse attitudes towards the topic which are held by teachers (see 'What the schools think', Chapter 2).

In our view, it is not always desirable to single out the topic for isolated consideration. It is often preferable to consider giftedness as one form of exceptionality. Simple labels for groups of children, such as 'the gifted', 'the less able', 'the academic' and 'the average', can lead to the belief that the characteristics of groups may be simply defined, that there are group syndromes, or that group provision can be made for children with particular needs. The group label 'gifted children' seems to have an emotive effect and can polarise viewpoints in a way not conducive to clear thinking about appropriate provision for the specific needs of individuals.

Ideally, we would hope to see a consideration of giftedness in the broader context of creating greater awareness of all forms of individual difference in a school.

Identification

Awareness of gifted children, in the context of considering individual differences, is heightened when a school has developed an effective procedure for identifying and recording such differences.

Although our visits revealed no complete model of identification procedure, we would like, on the basis of our experiences, to suggest that:

a. A sound identification procedure for gifted pupils should be a part of a programme of monitoring individual differences throughout the school.

b. A sound procedure for the identification of gifted individuals requires agreed baselines, definitions or sets of criteria upon which identification can be based. No baseline can be perfect, but that is no reason for a school not attempting to establish baselines. It is quite clear that the proportion of children which is identified as gifted varies widely. No debate about whether such variation is justified can be realistic unless the baselines are made explicit and known to other schools with which the school concerned has a working relationship, and to the LEA.

c. A sound procedure for identification accepts, in addition to agreed baselines (definitions, sets of criteria), any clue to giftedness from inside or outside the school. Inside the school, examples of pupils' work and subjective teacher opinion provide important clues. Some teachers are particularly skilled in the art of identifying high potential in children. Such teachers could be deployed beyond the confines of their own classroom or work areas (or even in other schools or in-service training courses) to help less experienced or less highly trained teachers to recognise the signs of giftedness.

Clues to giftedness that come from 'outside' the school and should be utilised might well include full and unambiguous records from contributory schools, parental views, and information about deep interests and extra-curricular activity.

d. A sound procedure for identification provides early and continued opportunities for giftedness to be revealed and noted. Early identification is said by some subject specialist teachers to be very important for certain special gifts. Early and continued identification can take place only if the criteria of giftedness are made explicit, if identifying teachers do their work effectively, and if the curriculum includes those activities for which early identification is essential. (For example, most music teachers insist upon the importance of early identification of talent.)

e. A sound procedure for identification is of limited use if the information is not recorded and used. Information must be accessible to teachers. It should be transmitted when a child changes school, updated regularly and used to check rate of progress and possible underachievement.

f. A sound procedure for identification uses what objective measures of ability it can. Standardised tests are of little use to a school if there is no teacher who can advise upon the use and value of standardised tests, show which can be used as diagnostic tests, select correctly, administer them and interpret scores. Each school would benefit from at least one such individual who can advise the school and liaise with LEA testing services. For this purpose, an individual may need appropriate in-service training for the role. Standardised tests (including individually administered tests of general ability) should be regarded as no more than one form of clue to giftedness.

LEAs can often assist with some kinds of identification of gifted children. Again, we feel that this should be in the context of noting individual differences in general, or exceptional differences of all kinds.

LEA psychological services have a great many demands upon their time, and therefore it is unrealistic to expect individual testing for more than a small percentage of pupils. If, however, a school administers a group intelligence test or any other kind of standardised test, after consultation with LEA psychologists, the results might then be used to check against achievement in certain subjects. Severe underachievement in everyday work, relative to high test scores, might be investigated by LEA psychologists who would then test for higher or more specific abilities. In other words, the testing load on a school psychological service, which has many other calls on its resources, can be relieved by close liaison with the school and progressive screening (see Testing programmes, Chapter 2).

LEA advisers may, and often do, have skills in the identification of specific forms of giftedness which are not amenable to objective testing. They can help schools to formulate criteria for giftedness in specific subject areas, and describe manifestations of gifted behaviour.

Some LEAs may wish to consider following the example of those who have already designated a coordinator of identification procedures and central resource provision for exceptional children. As a part of this broader role, such a coordinator (teacher, adviser, or LEA officer, according to local conditions) can encourage the development of definitions and sets of criteria for specific forms of giftedness, and arrange for interchange of information.

The coordinator might note, and try to account for, wide differences in the reported incidence of gifted children throughout an LEA. Where standard school records do not exist, the coordinator might explore with schools the ways in which the recording and transmission of information (see e. above) could become more effective. Opportunities might be created for teachers to see work with pupils with various forms of specific giftedness and to note different forms of provision. In addition to encouraging the identification of the exceptional child, the coordinator might have some responsibility for provision.

Provision—other institutions

While we believe that all middle and comprehensive schools have a responsibility to identify and to provide for the gifted child, it cannot be assumed in every case that the school will be able to make provision from its own resources. Where it cannot, the school should ensure that the responsibility for provision is taken up by another institution or agency. We do not think that any school or LEA should neglect to accept, or to delegate, responsibility for provision on the grounds that 'the gifted can look after themselves' or that 'to make provision for the exceptional is to do so at the expense of the unexceptional'. We look first at the possibility for provision by other institutions or agencies.

Transfer 'outward'. As a general rule, we would suggest that the establishment of special schools is not necessary for gifted pupils who are regarded as 'gifted all-rounders'. Such a policy of transfer implies a number of assumptions: that gifted pupils are gifted in all respects; that it is practicable to select such pupils with precision; that segregated forms of provision are preferable to unsegregated forms of provision. These assumptions need to be questioned.

There are schools which exist as institutions for those with specific gifts (for example in music or drama). Our remit did not extend to include visits to such schools. We think that before transfer to such schools takes place, those concerned should ascertain that the special school has a balanced curriculum as well as exceptional facilities for the support of a specific form of giftedness.

An alternative to the school for special gifts is the department in a comprehensive school which has developed exceptional facilities or expertise. In areas of dense population, transfer for a pupil from one comprehensive school to another which has a strong specialism may be a helpful form of provision within an LEA.

Early transfer to the next tier. When a child appears to be well ahead of his contemporaries in terms of achievement, a school may decide to allow him to transfer early to the next tier. This practice should take into account the all-round physical, social and intellectual development of the pupil. It presupposes that the substitution of one type of year for another can take place without harm. We believe that such a combination of conditions is rare, and think that LEAs and schools are right to be cautious in the use of upward transfer. Transfer, in itself, is not a sufficient form of provision for gifted pupils. In order to avoid anxiety, unhappiness or strain, the greatest care should be taken to ensure that the child is sufficiently mature in all respects to profit by the transfer. Pupils, heads of both schools, and parents should be in full agreement. LEA educational psychologists should give individual tests and teachers should be consulted for their views of present achievement and potential. Transfer should be followed up by monitoring of pupil progress.

Partial transfer. Complete transfer (either upward or outward) is not always desirable (as we indicated above) or possible, for a variety of reasons; receiving schools may be too far from the pupil's home, the receiving school may have strong provision in one subject but be weak in other respects, siblings may wish to attend the same school, and so on. The practical difficulties of transferring a child to another institution for a part of the week may be considerable, yet the principle seems to be one worthy of far closer examination, and possibly of wider implementation on an experimental basis. LEAs might encourage partial transfer between secondary and tertiary institutions.

However, any form of partial transfer is a practice which requires the most careful selection procedures and subsequent monitoring of the pupil's attainment across the curriculum, as well as his progress in the specific specialism of the school.

Federal appointments. As a possible alternative to the transfer arrangements listed above, and as a means of reducing the logistical problem of moving groups of pupils from school to school, LEAs might make federal appointments (one teacher appointed to two or more institutions). This is a means of enabling highly specialised teachers to be available to gifted pupils in a number of schools.

Provision—LEAs

In the section on identification above, it was suggested that LEAs may wish to designate individuals with responsibility for exceptional children. As a logical extension to the task of coordinating identification, such a person might well coordinate some aspects of LEA provision. For example, he or she might:

Designate, with the help of specialist teachers, school departments which have particularly good provision for the specific forms of giftedness and oversee movement of pupils to that department from other schools.
Liaise with teachers who have special responsibility for exceptional pupils and call regular meetings to review LEA provision.
Ensure that schools are aware of LEA policy and practice with regard to transfer, award of grants, movement of pupils to

specialist centres, use of federal appointments and in-service provision focused on exceptional pupils.

Keep a register of voluntary agencies which, and individuals who, might offer support for children with specific gifts.

Explore the possibility of joint provision with other LEAs.

However, we must point out that we do not think that the best provision is necessarily made by transfer, partial transfer, or through central LEA resources. A school must first review its own resources for provision.

Provision—in school

Streaming, setting and mixed ability grouping. We found little evidence to suggest that one form of grouping, in itself, was any more helpful to the gifted than another form. The form of pupil grouping a school wishes to adopt should be seen as the framework within which there must be differentiated work. Our suggestion on the matter would therefore be in the form of the caveat stated earlier (see In-school provision, Chapter 2): no form of class grouping is, in itself, adequate provision for gifted pupils.

Withdrawal. We hope that withdrawal of individual pupils from a class for the purpose of working alone, with a small number of other pupils, or with a teacher or other adult, is a practice which is not confined to the exceptional pupil. However, it can be a particularly useful form of provision for a gifted pupil. For example, there can be a dialogue with an adult or with other gifted children which might be inhibited in the group atmosphere of a classroom. We have no evidence to suggest that a gifted child is envied or ostracised when withdrawal takes place, but it is clearly better if withdrawal is as much a part of the everyday life of a class and all its members as resources will allow. We saw some excellent examples of the use of volunteer adult 'experts' who were prepared to visit the school to work with the children who had specific gifts, and would suggest that schools look closely at the possibility of contacting local helpers for this work, which can enrich and support the teacher's work.

Promotion and acceleration. Promotion has some of the advantages and disadvantages of 'early transfer', which is its logical sequel. We think that the practice of early promotion of a pupil to a higher age group for all his school work presupposes a degree of all-round giftedness, and physical and social maturity which a pupil may not possess. Acceleration, on the other hand, is a useful form of provision for children with specific gifts. A pupil can either work with an older and more advanced group or, in some cases, work on a self-teaching course.

Enrichment. We were often impressed by the way in which teachers enriched their work with gifted children. Enrichment is an activity which is a function of the teacher's flexibility, sensitivity to individual needs, mastery of subject area and sense of timing. It is therefore very difficult to find the appropriate kind of enrichment in text books, or other forms of commercially prepared curricular material. It is easy to underestimate a teacher's skill and capacity for extending pupils. There is often no necessity to resort to such practices as promotion and transfer when gifted pupils can be extended by expecting a high standard or level of abstraction to be reached.

Homework. Enrichment for gifted pupils can, in theory, take place by allotting them tasks which are more demanding. We recognise that it is a time-consuming matter to set and to mark individual tasks for homework which are geared to the needs of particular individuals. Nevertheless it was disappointing to find that gifted pupils (and those at the other extreme of the ability range) were so often given work which was qualitatively no different from that expected of the majority.

Libraries. The less than satisfactory situation regarding study space which we described in the section on libraries may be transitory. As school rolls fall and more teaching space is released for other purposes, we hope that libraries will be used for their proper purposes, and cease to double as teaching accommodation. Other released teaching space might also be used for quiet study as well as libraries, especially for sixth form work. Often the sixth form library is the only quiet place in a school for individual study and for this reason, unfortunately, younger pupils are excluded from library facilities which may be more appropriate to their needs.

Special equipment. Those areas of the curriculum which make use of special equipment present a particular problem, which we described earlier. Despite our reservations about transfer, this may be the only practical solution when highly specialised equipment is in short supply. If a school wishes to contain provision for gifted pupils, ad hoc arrangements can be made for a pupil to share the use of equipment with older or more advanced groups. However, in no case can it be assumed that a gifted pupil is able to operate specialist equipment with less supervision and safeguards than other pupils.

The curriculum

At middle school and lower secondary school level, pupils with general or specific gifts experience a balanced curriculum. However, at or after the third year of secondary schooling, imbalance occurs. Pupils with general gifts reduce their experience of the performance areas of the curriculum in favour of 'academically respectable' subjects. Teachers of art, music, drama and craft subjects complain that pupils with specific gifts in these performance areas are advised to concentrate upon academic subjects.

We agree with the general view expressed in schools that at least until the age of 16, all pupils, including the gifted, ought to experience a broad and balanced curriculum which does not exclude performance subjects. We believe that it is the responsibility of schools to ensure this balance, and that a pupil should not pursue his special gifts to the exclusion of other important areas of the curriculum.

We think that it is desirable and possible for the principle of balance to be sustained beyond the age of 16, although there will obviously be a narrowing and deepening of the curriculum content. Balance may be achieved by a sound programme of sixth form general studies, by a mix of major specialist and minor studies, or even by ensuring that the pupil has a broad range of extra-curricular experiences. Since education after 16 may take place in a variety of institutions, it may be that this balance can be sustained by other arrangements, including cooperation between school and further education institutions.

Type and size of school

It may seem surprising that we conclude that there is no direct relationship between a school's capacity to identify and to provide for gifted pupils, and the size and type of school. Such factors may be important but at present they are concealed by the fact that comprehensive schools are still at an early stage of evolution in the great majority of LEAs, that they sometimes do not have a complete ability range (there may be 'creaming off' to other schools), or that awareness or lack of awareness may be a function, predominantly, of local factors. Nevertheless, we note that in three tier systems, the transmission of records is more difficult, continuity of curricular content and level is broken twice, instead of once, and in such circumstances the identification and progress of gifted pupils may suffer. (In this they are no different from the other children in the system.) Factors such as school catchment area, age and dispersion of school buildings and the managerial skills found in the institution often outweigh questions of school size.

As a final point, we would suggest that schools guard against insularity, in the identification of, and possible provision for, exceptional pupils, by pooling teachers and physical resources. No school is so small or so large that it can be confident that it can operate more effectively by being independent of other schools and educational institutions. Groups of schools (where necessary with the help of the LEA coordinator for exceptional pupils, suggested above) may wish to consider arrangements for sharing staff who can help to identify and to provide for the gifted, and the possibility of pooling physical resources.

The gifted individual

The whole trend of our survey has been to note the necessity to talk about gifted children in the broad context of individual differences. Gifted children are like other children in one important respect; they are individuals and should not be thought of as a group, with common characteristics.

In order to meet their needs it is more useful to think of provision for particular aspects of giftedness, than to attempt to provide for general giftedness.

Appendix

Table 1 *The 132 middle and comprehensive secondary schools visited by or for the working party*

Age range	Number of pupils on roll	1–249	250–499	500–999	1000–1499	1500–1999	2000+	Totals
Middle schools		5	17	29				51
11–13, 11–14				4				4
11–16				10	5			15
11–18			1	11	28	8	5	53
12–18, 13–18					1	2		3
14–18				3	1		1	5
Sixth form college				1				1
						Grand total		132

Table 2 is drawn from information compiled during an HMI National Survey of maintained secondary schools of all types (NSS), which was conducted independently of our own survey. The complete NSS sample is 10 per cent (about 400 schools). At the time of compiling this data 182 schools had been visited of which 107 were named comprehensive schools (although this does not mean that all the schools in the sample had an intake which represents the full ability range). The small sample shows the number of schools which, on their own evidence, confirmed by HMI, try to identify pupils with 'superior intellectual ability' (upper 2 per cent of full ability range) or with specific gifts.

Table 2 *The identification of children with superior intellectual ability or with specific gifts*

	Number of schools surveyed	Schools which identify superior intellectual ability	Schools which identify specific gifts
11–16 comprehensive schools with a full range of ability	11	5	6
11–18 comprehensive schools with a full range of ability	28	18	21
13–18 comprehensive schools with a full range of ability	14	8	6
All comprehensive schools with a full range of ability (including those above)	54	33	34
All schools named 'comprehensive' including those with an intake of less than the full ability range	107	40	60

Glossary

Some of the terms used in this publication are in general use in educational discussion. A few, however, are our own stipulated definitions, which we use in the interest of brevity or clarity.

Acceleration
Covering a specific course of study faster than the other children. See also **Promotion.**

Assessment
The measurement or estimation of pupil ability or achievement. Assessment may range from standardised test results to class teacher estimates of attitude. See also **Test.**

Comprehensive school
One in which the admission of pupils is not based upon selection by reference to ability or aptitude.
For various historical or geographical reasons, comprehensive schools do not always have pupils representative of the full ability range. In the text our examples usually indicate where a school is comprehensive in name, but not in range and balance of pupil ability.

Contributory school
School from which pupils are sent to a higher **Tier** institution. Thus several primary schools may act as contributory schools for a secondary school. Sometimes termed **Feeder school.** See also **Receiving school.**

Differentiated work
School work which suits each pupil, rather than a standard task which a whole group is expected to perform.

District Inspector
One of Her Majesty's Inspectors of Schools who has a particular responsibility for liaison with a local education authority.

Elite
The term is used to imply belief in the selection and segregation of a small group of pupils with a view to preparing them for future high office in society.

Enrichment
General term for a change in quality of work to a level much higher than that normally expected of a particular age group. Enrichment materials purport to promote or support a higher level of thinking.

Exceptional child
Child at an extreme end of the ability range. In crude terms, the top or bottom 2 per cent of general intellectual ability. The term is sometimes extended to include the handicapped.

Extra-curricular activity
That which a school provides beyond a timetabled programme. Extra-curricular activities such as clubs or hobbies groups usually take place under the control of teaching staff, but outside normal school hours.

Federal appointment	An appointment of a teacher or lecturer to two or more educational institutions, often at more than one **Tier** or level. Thus a teacher may work in a **Middle school** and an **Upper school** in the same week. See also **Peripatetic teacher.**
Feeder school	See **Contributory school.**
Gifted child	Shorthand for any child who manifests one or more of the forms of ability described in Chapter 1.
Middle school	Literally, the 'middle school' in a three Tier education system. Usually middle schools span four years of some part of the middle years of schooling. (9–13 and 8–12 middle schools are the most common.) Occasionally middle schools are the second tier of four tier systems.
Middle years of schooling	Age 8 to 13. (Children in the middle years of schooling are not necessarily in **Middle schools.**)
Mixed ability classes	Where pupils of a wide range of ability and aptitude are taught together. See also **Sets, Streaming.**
Partial transfer	Where a pupil spends part of a school week in a school or educational institution other than that in which he receives most of his schooling.
Peripatetic teacher	One who is not attached to a particular school but who travels round serving two or more. Peripatetic teachers are appointed to an LEA, rather than a school or group of schools. See also **Federal appointment.**
Performance areas	Our own term, used here as shorthand for 'art, craft, physical education, music, home economics and drama'.
Promotion	The movement of an able pupil to a class above his/her chronological age. See also **Acceleration.**
Receiving school	Any school which takes pupils from one or more **Contributory schools.**
Setting	Arrangement of pupils, usually of a single age-group, into groups (sets) according to ability in a particular subject. Thus a child may be in the highest set for maths, the lowest for English and a middle set for modern languages. See also **Mixed ability classes, Streaming, Vertical grouping.**
Screening	A procedure applied to a group of children to determine if any meet a specified criterion (e.g. IQ in excess of 135). Screening is normally followed by some form of special provision for those who meet the criterion.
Streaming	Practice of dividing all the children of the same chronological age into separate classes on the basis of general ability. See also **Setting, Mixed ability classes.**

Talent Giftedness in an area of artistic or musical endeavour.

Tertiary institution Any educational institution such as a college or university which succeeds secondary schooling. Tertiary institutions operate under different regulations, staffing and financial arrangements from secondary schools. Thus a pupil may leave school at 16–plus to enter a college of further education (tertiary institution) or remain in an 11–18 school (secondary institution). (Tertiary colleges are tertiary institutions which are responsible for the 16–plus education of all students in a given area.)

Test A particular situation set up for the purpose of making an **Assessment**. Tests which are Objectively scored will have the same score, regardless of the scorer. Tests which are subjectively scored (for example, essays) are those where the marking may depend upon different interpretations by individual markers.

Testing programme The use of standardised tests at or after entry into a tier in the school system, for example the use of a reading score obtained in a national test as a part of achievement testing at the end of a primary school, prior to transfer to a secondary comprehensive.

Tier A distinct phase of schooling characterised by schools of one type. Each tier has different funding, staffing and pupil age group.
In this report we use the terms 'two tier' and 'three tier'. Four tier systems also exist, but we do not discuss them explicitly. In a two tier system of schooling a child makes one transition of school (usually from primary 6–11 to secondary 11–18). In three tier systems a child makes two transitions (for example 6–8 first school, 9–12 middle school, 12–18 upper school).

Transfer Removal of a pupil from one educational institution to another:
—**Outward**: removal to an institution whch is deemed to have more appropriate provision. For example a gifted child musician may transfer from one secondary school without a specialist music teacher to another which is seen to have a department with specialist teachers and an orchestra.
—**Upward**: removal of a pupil from one **Tier** to the next higher. Also termed **Early transfer**. (For example a primary school pupil with very high general ability and all-round physical and social maturity may transfer upward to the secondary school at age 10 instead of age 11.)

Upper school A school which caters for the oldest age group in a three tier education system. Usually an upper school takes pupils from a **Middle school.**

Whole class teaching Teaching at a particular level to the whole class rather than teaching at varied levels and paces to suit individual differences of pupils.

Withdrawal Temporary removal from a class in order to provide special tuition or other experiences appropriate to his needs. In secondary schools withdrawal is usually confined to **Exceptional** pupils.

Vertical grouping   Where pupils move upward through a school on the basis of achievement, regardless of their chronological age. Progression is from group to group, each of which consists of pupils of very similar attainment.

VR scores   Verbal Reasoning (VR) tests measure knowledge of words and ability to reason with words. The scores enable a pupil's performance in the **Test** to be evaluated in relation to that of other pupils of the same age.

Part II Some Views on Giftedness in School Subjects

1 Introduction

These papers on giftedness in a number of subjects and areas of the curriculum have been written by individual members of the working party, and other members of Her Majesty's Inspectorate. The papers draw on HMI experience of looking at these subject areas in schools and of working with teachers. In some cases, the papers have been accepted as a statement from the relevant subject committee in the Inspectorate; in others they represent the views of individuals. Part II is therefore significantly different from Part I of this report, and the papers which follow should be considered as discrete chapters.

The selection of subjects includes many of those found in the curriculum of the middle years of schooling, whether these are passed in a middle school or the lower years of a secondary school.

In each paper there is an attempt to outline the characteristics of giftedness as shown in that subject or curriculum area, a description of policies and methods used in the support and development of pupils with these gifts, and in some cases recommendations for the improvement of such provision are outlined. It is interesting that many of the recommendations for the improvement of the provision are recognised as improving the provision in that subject area for pupils of all abilities, and not only those gifted in the subject. Some conclusions and recommendations recur frequently in the different papers; these include the importance of:

—'good' teachers
—'adequate' resources
—provision for individual pupils
—involvement of individuals and agencies outside the school.

Although these topics have been examined in Part I, in these papers each is looked at with specific reference to a subject area, and details are given which draw a fuller picture of the meaning of such general phrases in the context of individual subjects.

In spite of the general similarity of structure shared by the papers, and the recurrence of some conclusions and recommendations reached in them, these papers on subject areas of the curriculum remain individual in approach and emphasis. We expect that they will be read as separate papers and we hope that each will provide a basis for discussion and action in the provision for gifted children in middle and comprehensive secondary schools.

2   Art

**Who are the
artistically gifted?**

Of those schools which are concerned at all, most seem to agree
about some common characteristics of artistically gifted children:

> They have an interest often amounting to an obsession with visual
> recording, matching the world around them to images which they
> create;
> they have an ability to depict in a way which is illuminating or
> revealing, seeing or emphasising unexpected relationships between
> colours or shapes;
> they either have, or readily acquire the draughtsmanship, manual
> and physical skills or techniques they need to convey their
> message. They are sensitive to the quality of the materials and
> tools they use. This is different from the facile competence some
> pupils have which is more concerned with the means than the
> message.

Artistically gifted children may show certain other highly regarded
characteristics, for example the ability to extrapolate readily from
experience, or a willingness to attempt alternative solutions to
problems set. They have an urge to work, with or without direction,
and the ability to persevere with a problem until its successful
completion, sometimes marked by a degree of obsessiveness. These
characteristics seem to be aspects of general intelligence and raise the
question of the relationship between artistic giftedness and general
intelligence—about which there is no agreed answer in schools. It
seems likely that most children with artistic gifts are also gifted in
other ways. However, there is good evidence that some pupils have
unmistakable artistic gifts even though their performance in other
respects is no more than average. Such differences of view may be
due to the fact that art depends for its effective expression on a
number of factors, on experience, on qualities of imagination, on
physical skills and on a degree of insight. It is not easy to outline the
boundaries of these factors and how they overlap with each other.
Some qualities may call for a high degree of general intelligence,
others less so, and schools emphasise these characteristics differently.

**Some examples of the
artistically gifted**

i. Colin, aged 13, at a large comprehensive school was quick in
conversation; his reaction to questions was sharp and wary. His
paintings stood out immediately (among work of a good general
standard) by virtue of accurate observation and painterly approach.
There was an emphasis on relationships rather than things-in-
themselves, a concentration on tone and colour rather than on shape
alone and an acceptance of the means, so that brush stroke remained
as brush stroke as well as tree or house. Colin was gifted in other
fields.

ii. Nicholas, a sixth former, was tough, boisterous, forceful. Art, one felt, was used as his means to impose his views, and his pictures are prominently signed. His work was used as a vehicle for his drive and desire to convert. A good draughtsman who produced strongly patterned pictures.

iii. James was quiet and shy and talented in art throughout his school career. Good in academic fields, painting strongly at 13, carving at 14, he showed an intense interest in art history in the sixth form. Filled many sketchbooks with his studies. Went to the Slade direct from school.

iv. Alex, aged 17, referred, with his twin, to the School Psychological Service for spelling and writing difficulties. General ability rating on the Stanford Binet Scale was 'average' with a notably wide scatter, ranging from failure on some items at the 12-year-old level and passing others at the superior Adult I level. Very able in art, he produced a varied folio which gained him admission to a major college a year early. He may have developed rapidly in visual terms as a result of his writing and reading frustrations.

How are gifted artists identified?

It would be very convenient if there were a generally agreed range of tests capable of assessing objectively the performance of pupils as artists. Instead much depends on the ability of a sensitive teacher and artist to recognise the degree and form of this quality in pupils. Most art teachers, perhaps as a result of the regular exercise of intuitive and visual judgements, feel confident in their own ability to recognise artistic giftedness without verbal definitions. Widely differing claims are made about the age at which giftedness can be identified. Some think it can be seen as early as 12 or 13 (there are few infant prodigies in this field), others feel that the sixth form, or less commonly the fourth and fifth years, are the earliest for recognition. A well-formulated judgement comes from a school which looks for 'the ability to relate symbols to reality' as the mark of emerging artistic giftedness. Art, it is claimed, like literature, demands the making of expressive judgements. Although some pupils have an early facility in depiction, and in the ability to organise visual qualities formally, these qualities have to be put to the service of discrimination, and this ability to form good judgements seems to be related to puberty. Real artistic giftedness can rarely, therefore, be identified much before 13.

Provision for the artistically gifted pupil

The rapid emergence of artistic ability after puberty is nonetheless dependent on having the skills and habits of work well formed before that age; in this respect the provision for many pupils in the middle years is not a happy one. Many, especially those in middle or intermediate schools, are without specialist help and important opportunities for the growth of skills and insights are lost. Few comprehensive schools make special arrangements (in the sense of special courses) for them, although many allow pupils who are interested to use studios in their own time. The pursuit of art takes time and the pressure upon pupils to devote their time to other studies, especially if they have multiple gifts, is intense. An equally sharp competition can prevail in the choice of options, or A-level courses. As in so many aspects of school life, the lead given by heads is crucial. In some schools the artistic are merely tolerated while in others they are cherished. Beyond this special function of the head in creating a sympathetic ethos, much depends on the sensitive awareness of individual teachers.

Only a few schools offer enrichment of the kind that can be found by contact with local artists, although many pupils visit museums or libraries, but gifted pupils often benefit from individual teaching in their schools—a distinctive feature of much art education. It is rare to find schools devoting extra money or resources to the artistically gifted although it must be said that, once identified, most pupils enjoy generous encouragement and guidance from their teachers. A few have help from outside the school. Some LEAs provide Saturday or weekend art classes in colleges of art or teachers' centres. These are notably successful devices for enlarging the experience of pupils, partly because of the challenge they offer of working with other enthusiasts, and partly because of the opportunities they sometimes provide of working with professional artists. The practice of art is for the most part a lonely, if rewarding, business and those who undertake it need supportive and enriching experiences of this kind. The development of the artist, it has been claimed, is proportional to the degree of his exposure to a variety of such influences. The role of the art teacher in the school remains nevertheless central and crucial.

Conclusions

What do artistically gifted pupils need from school? They need recognition first of all, and an acknowledgement that the gifts they possess do make them, not better or worse, but different. Then they need the opportunity—and sufficient time—to choose and to practise in their chosen field. Their practice and achievements should be challenged and appraised with vigour and frankness by teachers. There is no doubt about the beneficial effect on the artistically gifted of specialist teaching; its absence in many middle schools is a major hindrance to the early recognition of artistic talent and its development. Since schools with a strong general awareness of giftedness have little difficulty in finding very able pupils in fair number, it seems likely that there is much unrealised talent in less sensitive schools. For example there is an almost untapped reservoir of ability to construct and create in three dimensions—an underemphasised activity in most art departments. With an individual pattern of teaching, there is no special virtue in the segregation of the gifted, nor any special difficulty in teaching them in mixed ability groups—provided the teacher is aware of the need to extend gifted children. They need an enriching environment—an introduction to the culture and history of their chosen art, access to books and periodicals in variety for study in breadth, travel to galleries and museums, the opportunity to meet adult and experienced practitioners of their art, and the chance to work side by side with other gifted pupils in outside clubs or classes. If the course offered is individual and has imaginative potential, then the gifted flourish and develop. They need the right opportunities to go on doing this. Career guidance is patchy in quality and often parents of the gifted are unaware of the wide range of excellent opportunities open to someone with artistic gifts. All these are elements of good teaching of art in schools. But there is also a more passive element, a question of ethos. Schools should be enabling places where idiosyncrasies are at least tolerated; to some extent originality depends on the freedom to be original.

3   Classics

What is giftedness in classics?

Giftedness in classics can take a variety of forms. For many years gifted students of Latin and Greek have fallen, broadly speaking, into two categories: the philologists, those with a flair for the subtleties of language in terms of grammatical and syntactical complexity; and the literary critics, those whose excellence of perception lies in sensitivity to literary form, the nuances of words and associations with or allusions to works either within or outside a given literary genre. Many of the most outstanding students have combined excellence in both these categories. The development over the past ten years of classical studies (courses about the classical world without the study of Latin or Greek) and therefore the accessibility of these studies to pupils whose gifts may not be in the narrow sense linguistic has increased the scope of classics and encouraged the emergence of giftedness similar to that of the historian, the student of art and the English literary critic, as described elsewhere in this document.

Among these varied forms, several characteristics are common: enjoyment of, even excitement about subtlety and complexity; a swift grasp of meaning and clarity of expression orally and in writing; accurate insights, intuitive and well informed, into another culture despite the differences in its attitudes and thought forms from our own; the mental energy to go beyond the merely adequate 'answers' of his or her peers which satisfy the teacher at any given stage to a depth of understanding which, despite the difficulties and intense concentration this involves, gives more personal and intellectual satisfaction. Specific aspects of giftedness in classics include the ability to translate idiomatically as well as correctly either from or into Latin or Greek, fluency and accuracy in the pronunciation of the classical language, skill in unravelling linguistic structures and tracing the derivation or associations of words, clear analysis of historical cause, effect and change, a reasoned response to literature and powers of discrimination between works of quality.

How is giftedness in classics identified?

Pupils rarely these days take Latin or Greek as a matter of course; they normally opt into them during their secondary school career, if indeed such subjects are on the timetable. The climate of opinion for various reasons seems to have moved against traditional subjects, and classics courses, on offer in only 47 per cent of comprehensive schools, very often have to contend with inadequate time allowances and minimal provision of other resources. Gifted children who might in different circumstances have had the opportunity of studying classics may be denied this or deterred from it, or of course attracted away from classics by a variety of alternative and worthwhile options in which their talents can be exercised. Potential in classics is often identified in pupils' aptitude for French, English or mathematics, while their degree of excellence emerges within the classics course. Giftedness is similarly revealed among those who undertake various courses in classical studies; here they are initially identified both by the enthusiasm they show for the ancient world and by the combination of clarity, neatness, flair and originality in their response to the material offered to them.

What provision is made?

Certain types of secondary reorganisation make any provision for classics difficult to achieve but whatever the type, time allowances below the sixth form are often only barely sufficient to enable the essentials of the course to be covered; in the atmosphere of haste there is therefore little opportunity for 'frills', indeed for any special provision for the gifted. Classics courses, linguistic or otherwise, are by no means the sole preserve of exceptional pupils, but the later such courses are provided in the secondary school, not only the later does giftedness in classics emerge but scope for its development (especially where Latin and Greek are concerned) may then be correspondingly reduced. Adoption of a common curriculum may militate against the inclusion of any classical courses before the fourth year but two or more periods per week may be found by limited withdrawal from appropriate subjects like English and French; such exceptional arrangements for the linguistically most able are considered by HMI to be as sound a practice as those for the least able, with the additional advantage that the most able are likely to suffer much less (if at all) from the loss of periods elsewhere. This time allocation is sometimes supplemented by additional periods blocked for a Latin/German/classical studies/remedial studies option for example. In some schools, special provision takes the form of either an extended day (a 'twilight' period once or twice a week), or time found within the lunch hour for any pupils who wish to extend their interest beyond what the normal timetabled provision allows, not just for pupils of a high calibre. Especially in schools where the classical sixth form no longer exists and where there is a demand for Greek or another classical subject from a very small group or even a single pupil, teachers also readily give up their non-teaching time during the school day to provide for them.

Where possible, teachers suggest pupils prepare more work ahead but this is normally only further reading of the text with which the whole set is concerned. Oral questioning is often angled to bring out the gifted. Sometimes a project or task involving some independent discovery work is included in the programme, and gifted pupils may occasionally be challenged to show their mettle in an unusually difficult essay question on background material, for example. Enthusiastic teachers loan their own books or obtain other books on loan, and where travelling distances and facilities happen to make this feasible, organise evening, weekend, or holiday visits to archaeological sites, exhibitions or lectures given by 'dons' in the local adult or school branch of the Classical Association. The most thorough-going provision is made by the annual summer school in Greek, organised by the Joint Association of Classical Teachers in Cheltenham, for people interested (beginners or at a more advanced stage) over the age of 16; the value of this experience is specifically recognised by both Oxford and Cambridge Universities as a qualification for undertaking the study of Greek within a degree course, and large numbers attend. At this summer school, gifted linguists, starting from only a knowledge of the Greek alphabet, are reading Homer and Plato by the end of a fortnight's intensive work. A substantial number of them are known to have gone on to read classics at university. At least four other summer courses, residential or non-residential, are also occurring in different parts of the country on an annual basis, bringing gifted senior pupils into contact with university teachers, very able school teachers and each other, to pursue the concentrated study of Latin or Greek. Members of an otherwise isolated minority group scattered over a wide area appreciate the stimulus of contact with one another and with the breadth and depth of university scholarship; for their teachers, though they are provided with more time and opportunity to extend individual pupils within the sixth form timetable than in the years prior to O-level at 16, the course is a welcome compensation for the necessity frequently to work as solo specialists with no other colleagues in their department with whom to share strengths, experience and judgement.

Some conclusions and recommendations

In general, therefore, opportunities for studying classics should not be denied to able pupils. Where such opportunities exist, the conditions under which classics teaching takes place need improvement. This is particularly so in the years when adequate opportunities must be provided if talents, especially linguistic talents, are to emerge in time to be nurtured up to A-level. Option systems call for closer attention to avoid subject groupings inimical to classical subjects. Excessively severe examination standards in comparison with other subjects should be acknowledged and lowered, since through assuming the participation of the ablest pupils, such standards can nevertheless progressively deter them. School libraries need to provide material for pupils whose interest has been aroused in classical subjects to read well beyond what is required by the examination syllabus or a particular course of study in the normal school curriculum. Old stock should be removed and replaced by new and up-to-date books, some exploring links with other European literature, art and architecture.

4   English

What is giftedness in English?

Giftedness in English may take many forms, some more recognisable than others. Academically, the pupils gifted in English show an unusually sensitive response to, and understanding of, literature, which grows and develops as their reading widens and their experience deepens. Along with this they have a mature and sustained capacity to express their responses and analyse the literary and linguistic means which have produced them. They have an ability to see beyond the particular to the general, to understand the nature of metaphor, to see the likeness between unlike things.

Creatively, the gifted pupils show an unusual capacity for organising in language their responses, feelings, ideas and thoughts in ways that convey those feelings and thoughts to the reader, and inform them with interest and excitement. At a very young age, such pupils will probably delight in playing with language and will have the ability to surprise the discerning ear by the originality, wit and vividness of the spoken word.

Some forms of giftedness in English are more surely recognised and valued in the outside world than in the educational context. The oral mode is a particular example; in the world outside it can be a powerful force, showing itself in such gifts as agility in argument, relevance in dialogue, fluency, ease and persuasiveness in spoken exposition, and the ability to move from one appropriate register to another as the occasion demands.

These wider manifestations of giftedness in English will also include an outstanding ability to read with understanding an increasing range and complexity of texts; and to write logically, accurately and clearly in the various expository as well as creative modes. It is important to recognise the variety of giftedness in English, as there is not enough evidence that the forms of giftedness are correlated with one another.

How is giftedness in English identified?

Most English teachers claim that they are able to recognise giftedness or very high ability in their pupils, often at early stages, though they make no precise distinction between these attributes. They see as critical the ability of the teacher to recognise the signs and nurture the growth points. Not all English teachers and departments have the resources to recognise and provide for all forms of giftedness in English. One very good department which fosters a study of poetry as central to its curriculum along with a continuing encouragement to the pupils to write in personal modes pays almost no attention to the development of oral skills. Another which develops writing skills with some success provides an arid diet of literature. Ideally, identification should be made possible by an English department which has a range and balance of interest and expertise.

Testing is rarely used to identify the gifted in English. Reading-age tests are mainly administered to indicate poor or non-readers.

Some schools, which test all entrants, do alert English teachers to pupils with high reading scores, as an indication of English potential. But such diagnosis of performance remains at a crude level, and is seldom the basis, say, for individual or group programmes which aim systematically at extending reading skills. The Bullock Report, *A Language for Life,* demonstrates the limitations of tests. It examines the three aspects of the teacher's work: to know the pupil; to know about the reading process; to know the possible range of reading available at a given time.

It may be worth noting that giftedness in English may reveal itself in subjects other than English. Written work of quality produced in subjects such as history or social studies, particularly before sixth form level, may derive as much from a capacity to handle language effectively as it does from an understanding of the concepts involved. It is difficult and undesirable to disentangle the medium from the message, but observation in schools suggests that subject teachers need the sensitivities and expertise of English specialists' responses to children's work if they are to develop the language ability inherent in such work.

As already suggested, some valuable manifestations of giftedness in English are not highly rated by many schools, and, therefore, fail to be identified. The ethos of the school itself may militate against development of some kinds of oral giftedness. On the other hand, schools have been visited where opportunities are contrived, within and outside the classroom, to give orally gifted pupils a variety of real situations in which to practise and extend their skills, for example oral presentations of scientific investigations, critical listening to taped discussions, carefully prepared interviews of visits. The school's general policy, and in particular the head's lead, seem crucial in this context, particularly in creating a favourable climate for development.

It might seem fair to conclude that the identification of giftedness in English is, and perhaps should be, almost wholly based on teachers' subjective assessments. The diversity of such giftedness demands a similar diversity of teachers. Chance plays a decisive part. Meaningful records, in the form of examples of pupils' work, are too seldom passed from primary to secondary schools. It seems certain that inherent giftedness may not be identified, unless the opportunity is created for linguistic gifts to be shown and to be recognised, in whatever form they appear.

What provision is made?

Identification precedes provision and as already suggested, the English teacher is critical to this issue. In large English departments, it is often a matter of chance which teacher a given pupil will meet, at all events before the sixth form and especially in the middle years of schooling; and in small departments, the range of interest and expertise required is not always available. Internal records and communications are vital to the consistent development of growing needs. Such need for coordination is sometimes met within large departments by forms of organisation which allow flexibility of grouping derived from block timetabling numbers of pupils and staff together.

The concealed shortage of English specialists ought also to be mentioned here. Many reports by HMIs comment on the lack of English specialists teaching the subject, or the absence of suitably qualified heads of departments. The Bullock Report makes the same point. Opportunities for the development of literary insights, for the offering of a range of textual challenge, and for a systematic widening and deepening of linguistic experience, must be lost to pupils in these circumstances. The head of one strong English department said that his main task with his most academically gifted pupil was to suggest the right book at the appropriate moment, to hint at a different approach from time to time, and then to leave him alone. This simple strategy concealed a professional awareness and knowledge that was essentially specialist.

It must also be said that a substantial number of English teachers and departments react strongly against the notion of giftedness. Systematic identification and special provision are assailed as a return to selective forms of elitism. Where resources are scarce it is preferred that they should be used at the other end of the ability spectrum. Time, energy and money are understandably invested in pupils with an insecure grasp of basic skills. It has already been remarked, however, that a skilful teacher can brief a gifted pupil in a few minutes for working on his own for some considerable time.

Where giftedness or special ability is an acceptable notion, the provision made is often limited to the opportunities offered by General Certificate of Education O-level and A-level courses. Even in his first year the bright pupil may be described as 'potential Advanced Level material'. One school which ended its first seven years of reorganisation with an Oxbridge scholarship in English divides the first year pupils into O-level and Certificate of Secondary Education bands on entering the school. A number of accelerated courses can be found of groups taking English language at O-level in the fourth year, or special O-level literature courses which are not offered to most pupils.

Provision for gifted pupils in English in mixed ability classes may have both advantages and disadvantages arising from this form of organisation. Courses and materials devised for individualised learning can provide them with open-ended opportunities that stretch and challenge. There is room for choice, and space for the private activities of reading and writing. On the other hand, mixed ability's frequent concomitant, a thematic approach to content, may deprive them of the experience of complete literary and other texts. Choice may be offered but not taken; and the group activity which explores essential meanings and understandings through collective discussion at a challenging level may be absent.

Opportunities offered outside the classroom are general and various. There are many drama groups, presentations and theatre and cinema visits, although these are not offered specifically or solely to gifted pupils. Some schools have writers' groups, often self-selective, and sometimes self-sufficient. Many professional writers visit schools under the 'Writers in Schools' scheme. A very few schools have resident writers for varying periods. A plethora of magazines, formal and informal, permanent and ephemeral, offer an audience to young writers. Good library-resource centres, and school book-shops, all provide opportunities.

Outside the school, apart from opportunities in drama, there is little specific support for gifted pupils. Some collections of children's poetry have been sponsored by local authorities and other agencies. Children's librarians often work closely with schools in encouraging the use of their wider book resources. Saturday and holiday drama, and Theatre in Education projects abound. But these are all generally available. There have been few initiatives, as in some other subjects, to bring together pupils gifted in English to give them appropriately exciting and stimulating experiences. There is some evidence that parental support and interest are critical.

Some conclusions and recommendations

i. Identification needs to be less haphazard and more precise. The particular aspect of giftedness in English, as recognised by a teacher at any stage, needs to be identified and recorded. Examples of work might usefully be included in records. Linguistic ability may show itself in any context, so all teachers are involved. Some kind of generally agreed school procedure is useful, as high ability in language may well be identified through other than English activities. Formal tests are crude instruments with limited powers, but they may be used as indicators of underachievement. The element of chance is real, and its effects require purposeful mitigation. There is a need, as pointed out in the Bullock Report, for the understanding of language to be acquired by all teachers during initial training, and for a fully specialist English teaching force.

ii. There is considerable evidence in HMI reports on English subject departments that very bright pupils are at a disadvantage in mixed ability classes. Departmental meetings have been attended by HMI where the problem posed to the department has been 'how to stretch the most able in mixed ability groupings'. Many English teachers are aware of this problem and are looking for solutions. Withdrawal is not favoured on social grounds. The organisation should allow opportunities for bright pupils to work together, for genuine discussion of work at their level with the teacher and for differentiation of materials and tasks so that they are challenged and stretched. In many schools, extra 'remedial' help is being brought into the classroom. Perhaps this might work for the most able too.

iii. Good resources are essential. A well-stocked library in itself is not enough. Bright pupils, in common with all pupils, need advice and encouragement to extend their range: the appropriate text at the right moment is all-important. Systematic extension of reading skills and broadening of experience make very considerable demands on teachers' own skills and knowledge.

iv. The teacher's role is all-important. Gifted pupils make demands of a special kind, just as slow-learning pupils do. The crucial issue is to find acceptable ways of bringing the appropriate pupils and teachers together—or even to make sure that the appropriate teachers are in the schools to begin with.

5   Geography

Some children show giftedness in specific ways such as by their facility in using language effectively in both the spoken and written modes, or in harnessing mathematical methods, skills and techniques to solve particular problems. But children who show particular aptitude in geographical studies will need to bring together a wide range of intellectual skills, some drawn from other disciplines, and others which are more particularly geographical in character and which are unlikely to be nurtured by any other disciplinary approach.

An important shift of emphasis has occurred in the discipline during the last twenty years. In contrast with the earlier concentration in geographical teaching on the uniqueness of places, the identification and description of regions and the building up of a body of geographical knowledge, now there is emphasis on attempts to identify and explain recurrent spatial patterns, processes and relationships, both physical and human; to develop a more scientific approach to explanation which may involve both generalisation and prediction; and to achieve a greater understanding of the complexity and delicate balance of relationships in the environment.

To achieve these objectives, the geography teachers will need to nurture some aspects of giftedness which may manifest themselves more immediately in other disciplines, as well as emphasising the subject's particular contribution in the development of concepts associated with the location of phenomena in space, and the analysis of the relationships which exist between man and his environment.

i. In seeking to identify pupils gifted in geography, the teacher will be concerned with the pupils' ability to observe accurately and to select or reject information which is relevant or irrelevant to a particular investigation. By virtue of the subject's emphasis on fieldwork as an essential element in the collection of raw information, pupils who are particularly accurate in observation, selective in the information collected, and refined in the method of recording can be quickly identified.

ii. The physical and man-made environments which are the raw material of the geographer present innumerable examples of regularities and patterns of location, distribution, links and movements. Gifted pupils will be those who, among other things, quickly recognise a distribution pattern and its significance in relation to causal factors; who recognise the presence of a significant pattern, relationship or process in several seemingly unlike examples such as the similarity between the steel industry at Consett and that at Ebbw Vale in terms of location, causation, current changes and prognosis; who comprehend more complex features on a macro-scale, for example drainage patterns, regions with a group of similar characteristics; and who can recognise and analyse a city as a complex of patterns of distributions and movements. Equally, gifted pupils will be quick to isolate the exception to the general pattern and will wish to seek and explain the reasons underlying the variation.

iii. Gifted pupils will be likely to question the validity and the limitations of the secondary source material with which they are required to work, for example texts, maps, aerial photographs, statistics. Are these adequate for the purpose? What other information would be likely to illuminate and broaden the scope of the investigation? How can it be obtained? How should it be used? The ability to select and adduce evidence from a wide range of sources will characterise gifted geography pupils.

iv. The control and management of resources, the problems of large cities, of developing countries, of over-population, of the use of hostile environments, and of the maintenance of environmental quality are subjects of present and likely future concern. Gifted pupils are likely to show an interest in and pursue in depth such questions as 'What are the likely consequences of particular courses of action? What hypotheses can be formulated relative to these questions? What kinds of experimental investigation will be necessary to test them? What degree of precision is required both in terms of measurement and of statement? What criteria do we use to evaluate the information?'

v. When all the information necessary to an investigation has been collected and analysed, the particular skill of gifted pupils will manifest itself in the command of language, of mathematical and of representational skills to make an ordered, reasoned argument in either the oral or written mode on the basis of which generalisations can be formulated.

What provision is made?

It would not be an exaggeration to say that, with very few exceptions, schools make little provision in terms of geography teaching for the gifted pupil. There is an increasing emphasis on teaching the subject to pupils in mixed ability classes and in many schools the subject is subsumed within an amalgam of disciplines, the academic purpose of which it is difficult to define. The teaching problems posed by these patterns of organisation are difficult and tax the ingenuity and skill of the teacher to such a degree that in many cases gifted pupils do not have the opportunities and encouragement to develop their particular aptitudes. Many courses fail to incorporate a sufficiently wide range of the many investigations more fully outlined above, which would enable the more gifted to exercise their talents.

Several agencies such as the Geographical Association, university departments of geography, polytechnics and local education authorities arrange one-day conferences for sixth form geography pupils. These meetings usually take a geographical theme of broad general interest and within this framework develop detailed studies related to A-level syllabuses and to recent research projects. In this way, gifted pupils, among others, are encouraged to think more widely and deeply and are made aware of the many and diverse areas of study which are available to intending students in higher education. This whetting of appetites is invaluable in stimulating pupils to think about the wider implications of their subject and in facilitating the interchange of ideas and interests between gifted geography pupils who may be isolated in their own schools.

Conclusions

In the past, when geography was often equated with memorising factual information, ability was regarded as being synonymous with a good memory. Good recall may be an attribute of giftedness but schools now need to do more to identify and nurture pupils of high geographical ability. To achieve this end it is necessary to devise a programme which will be increasingly demanding in terms of the complexity of ideas presented, the analytical procedures to be used, and in the degree of precision required, both in terms of the information to be used and of the statements to be made.

Another of the major tasks of a school is to ensure that the resources necessary for wide-ranging geographical investigations are available, such as texts, maps, aerial photographs, statistical sources, illustrative material, equipment for measuring and recording in the field. Without these the work undertaken is likely to be restricted to generalised textbook information; whereas with a range of resources, pupils' horizons can be broadened and a deeper insight into difficult problems made possible.

The teacher's role is a critical one and there is a clear need for schools to be staffed from the early years of secondary education with teachers both knowledgeable in the subject and aware of the potential of geography teaching for extending the intellectual abilities of these particularly able pupils.

6   History

History is a very accessible and amenable subject. It is not protected by complex technical vocabulary or by formulae; its assumptions are not tested in laboratories. Nor do many young people need to be coaxed or dragooned into an interest in the past—their comics, television viewing and many of their traditional games are evidence of a natural interest. The best of school history teaching often exploits this enthusiasm, uniting a wide range of ability in a common pleasure in the subject. Nevertheless, by the ages of 15 and 16 school history is too often seen merely as a matter of accumulating and memorising facts; skills and understanding play an insignificant role. To the school, a gifted child may be simply one who remembers most.

What is giftedness in history?

First, there are some necessary characteristics. Gifted historians whether they are 8 or 18 are likely to reveal themselves not so much by what they know as by what they do. Above all, they are likely to enjoy accumulating knowledge by reading. Pupils in the history class who are not 'bookworms' are unlikely to become gifted historians. They must surely seek to own, devour and value books; delight in reading is likely to be allied to a pride and pleasure in memorising what they read.

They may also be collectors of stamps, coins, matchboxes, cheese labels, post cards and other objects. They may in their spare time be keen visitors to museums, castles, country houses, and observers of the behaviour of their contemporaries or of television programmes with an historical interest. But these activities in themselves need not be significant pointers to the potentially gifted historian unless they are allied to persistent reading.

But history is not just the progressive accumulation of facts and the ability to remember them. The activities we have so far described are necessary but not sufficient criteria for identifying a potentially gifted historian. History is concerned with the activities of people who have actually lived, or indeed who may still be alive. It is a discipline which depends on an inescapable and crucial link between statements about people and evidence. But historical evidence is never complete, and is often subject to a variety of distinct but equally valid interpretations. Thus historical statements are always tentative and provisional. They can be judged only by criteria of consistency—consistent with the available evidence, and plausibility—plausible in the light of what we know and have experienced of human behaviour. Potentially gifted history pupils are unlikely to be able to formulate their interest in the past in this way, but their attitudes and patterns of thought can anticipate genuine patterns of historical thinking. Thus the test is not the pupils' ability to accumulate knowledge, but what they do with it.

Pupils who ask: 'Please sir, how do we know you are telling us the truth?' may not be impertinent; they are posing a crucial question which an historian can ask. They are aware that statements about people depend for their validity on the authority and type of available evidence, whether it is their teacher's statements, their textbooks, a document, a newsfilm, or a photocopy of their parish register.

History also reminds us constantly of the complexity behind the apparent simplicity of many human actions. It reminds us that heroes and heroines, like good and bad kings, are unhistorical simplifications imposed on the past. Thus children who are likely to become gifted historians begin to distribute their sympathies and realise that there is something to be said for the Indians, that they are not sure whether they are Saxons or Normans: older pupils may question the relationships between, say, freedom and democracy, or progress and improvement. Gifted pupils are readily able to accept and perceive the doubt that must lurk in the middle of all apparent certainties and begin to reveal that most important of an historian's intellectual qualities: informed scepticism.

But there is a third element every bit as important as evidence, that is, imagination, the ability of an historian to enter into a degree of informed and compassionate identification with the predicaments and points of view of other people. Mature historians will talk of 'empathy'. Younger children ask questions like: 'What was it really like in the last war daddy?' 'What would I have done . . .?' 'What was it like to be Caesar, or Drake, or Hitler, or a Jarrow hunger marcher, or my great-grandfather?'

Thus our pupils with their potential for giftedness in history may not be very easy members of the history class. They may not want to take much for granted; they may seek to question and constantly to challenge; acceptable explanations may seem over-simple to them. The books and tasks within the classroom may be insufficient to satisfy their curiosity, and the demands of homework and examination answers may seem to come between them and their own enthusiasms. They may be too easily dismissed as trouble-makers or eccentrics. Furthermore, their ability to communicate their ideas in writing or verbally, if they have not been defeated into taciturnity, may be confused. It is possible that their ability to identify questions and to explore ideas will be far in advance of their technical ability to express them clearly.

The encouragement of giftedness

The characteristics we have so far identified are in no way predictive. They raise the possibility rather than define the certainty of giftedness.

Potentially gifted historians will still lack a final essential requirement—the ability to communicate, to give their material shape and purpose in the form of narrative. Gifted pupils may need as much guidance in the clarity and accuracy of expression as their less able contemporaries.

So a school must first recognise the possibility of the existence of giftedness. Second, it must train pupils in the organisation and categorisation of information, and particularly in the skills of clear and accurate expression, written and oral. We have said nothing so far in this paper about skills and concepts. An increasing number of teachers of history are now relating the content of their history syllabuses to a series of increasingly demanding skills and increasingly complex concepts. It would be quite wrong to suggest that this kind of syllabus, or history societies designed to support specialist enthusiasms for that matter, should be aimed particularly at gifted pupils. They should support the learning and interests of all pupils. But a scheme of work that does not seek to define a hierarchy of skills and a development in understanding is unlikely either to identify, let alone challenge and enthuse, the most gifted members of the history class.

There are, of course, some habits of thought which require more than average ability. They may include argument by analogy, the ability to extrapolate, the ability to make comparisons between societies in different periods of history or between dissimilar societies existing at the same time, the ability to detect bias and prejudice, and the ability to construct and test hypotheses. Gifted pupils may not necessarily reveal any natural propensity to think within these patterns but it will be the teacher's responsibility to encourage them and to train their effective expression. Of course these ways of thinking are not exclusive to history, but pupils are unlikely to demonstrate real giftedness in history unless they are able to work within them and, what is of great importance, work within them with delight.

Third, it must meet the demands of external examiners. Here some compromise is unavoidable. Gifted pupils may well resent the limited opportunities which examination syllabuses give them to pursue their specialist interests, or to challenge the over-simplifications which lie at the heart of many questions, or which are simply boring because of the limited skills required of them. Nevertheless, there are syllabuses which, in part at least, give greater scope to the gifted pupil. There are opportunities within O- and A-level syllabuses for pupils to act as detectives, to analyse problems, to formulate and test hypotheses, to submit dissertations and to discuss the methods of historians, including their own. Thus schools which seek to serve giftedness must be prepared to spend some time in discovering the variety of examination possibilities, and to accept the problems arising from administering examinations from more than one board within a single school.

Fourth, a school must provide promising material, as well as time, and a place for talk and discussion. Above all, promising material is likely to be books. Gifted children will seek a greater variety and complexity of reading than they are likely to discover in most of their class books. They may well demand opportunities for sustained reading on specialist topics. But their reading habits need to be guided and stretched. An obligation to quote sources and to construct bibliographies encourages gifted pupils to seek their own information; pupils who use a book not suggested by the teacher are a credit to them both. There is no reason why home and classwork should not oblige pupils to consult the resources of the public as well as the school library.

But opportunities for sustained pleasurable reading depend not only on the existence of books but on a place and a time for reading. Classroom organisation and syllabus planning which does not allow individuals on occasions to pursue their eccentricities and enthusiasms may blunt giftedness. Libraries used as classrooms cannot be centres for study, research and thought. Upper school libraries which are closed to the gifted middle and lower school pupils will discourage and not stimulate.

Gifted pupils also need to talk and discuss. Talk gives an opportunity not only for pupils to develop and demonstrate their ideas but it provides an opportunity for the teacher to give those ideas shape and coherence.

Thus many gifted children may need a more flexible and relaxed policy on work and the acceptance of a different kind of relationship with their teacher. Gifted history pupils may know more, have perceived more and investigated a greater variety of sources than their teacher. To the perceptive teacher, this will be a measure of his success, not of his shortcomings.

There are of course a number of other activities which cannot easily be contained within a classroom and school library. Activities such as classical and industrial archaeology, war games, and documentary drama may be more easily pursued in school clubs and societies. It is of course possible to pursue some of these, as is the collecting of stamps or old post cards or second-hand books, in isolation and at home, but the young gifted historians may need the immense benefit of fellow enthusiasts and on occasions of an audience. A history department should also have easily available information about organisations and societies which encourage the enthusiasms of the gifted at weekends and during holidays.

7   Mathematics

Quickness at figures has long been regarded as one of the main
indicators of mathematical ability. From some points of view,
calculation is by no means the beginnings of mathematics, but it has
often been the point at which the gifted displays phenomenally rapid
growth and it is easily recognised by the layman. It is certainly an
asset for a mathematician to be quick at figures but beyond a certain
point it ceases to give much further benefit, and able mathematicians
are characterised by their ability to avoid tedious calculations even
more than by their ability to perform them. The arrival of the pocket
calculator changes the perspective once more. Nowadays, the able
7-year-old who is set an investigation which involves extensive
calculation may arrive next day with a borrowed pocket calculator,
and turn in a thoroughly competent job.

Some young mathematicians first indicate their talents by their
skill at geometry. Infants may show this by an unusual ability with
bricks, or by making patterns in art, or by their skill with logi-
blocks. Initially this may be intuitive, but later the young mathematicians stand apart from the young artists by their ability to
verbalise their experiences and to discuss what would happen if the
conditions were varied. Over recent years, the amount of geometry
in primary schools has increased; thus the opportunities for the
gifted to develop and the responsibilities on the teacher to appreciate
what is happening have increased correspondingly. At the same time
in secondary schools the amount of formal, deductive geometry has
dramatically declined. For many years, skill in deductive geometry
was a reliable indicator of future potential. The case for changing the
geometry syllabus in secondary schools was very strong, but can we
be sure that current geometry teaching challenges the able as it did,
and as it still should?

Mathematics today is more wide ranging and varied than ever
before, and it offers scope for a corresponding diversity of talent.
The ability to calculate and the ability to reason about geometrical
shapes were traditionally signs of mathematical giftedness; are there
other less explicit indicators?

Mathematical potential may be revealed by beautifully precise
communication. Gifted pupils can have a wide vocabulary and a gift
for selecting the appropriate word. Their language may be impres-
sively concise as well. They may reveal themselves in other ways—
the original remark, the unexpected question, the leap to the abstract,
the distrust of intuition, a persistence and desire for perfection. They
may detect ambiguity or imprecision in the teacher's mathematical
language.

Gifted young mathematicians want to generalise, set the particular
fact in a general setting, relate one problem to another quite different
one. What will happen, they will ask themselves, or their friends, or
a teacher:

—if we change the numbers?
—if we work in a different base?
—if we used letters instead of numbers?
—if we turned it upside down, or reflected it, or enlarged it?
—if we did it in three dimensions instead of two?
—if we tried it with irregular figures as well as regular ones?
—if we imagined it drawn on a balloon?

Most mathematics teachers will have encountered such queries, and anyone who has not might perhaps ask himself whether his approach unwittingly discourages them.

There may also be a delight in logical fantasy; it is no coincidence that Lewis Carroll was a mathematician. Mathematicians often play chess and they are often musical, acquiring a wide general knowledge and perhaps performing competently on an instrument.

Provision for the mathematically gifted

In former times, provision for the gifted mathematician was most often automatic in the sense that the pupils were setted or streamed for the teaching of mathematics, and the ablest were with their peers and received more demanding material than was given in other classes. This continues in many schools, but if by 'gifted' we mean the ablest 2 per cent then it can be seen that even with this system of organisation the gifted are still unlikely to be taught with many of their peers. By their standards, most of their classmates are mediocre, and if the school employs a style of teaching which uses the same material for the whole of the class, hopefully pitching it round about the middle, then the gifted are still unstretched. Whatever the form of school and classroom organisation, the talents of the gifted in mathematics can only be matched if there is some measure of individuality in the work they are expected to do.

Mathematics can fail to stretch the gifted in a particular way of its own. Most mathematical exercises contain a built-in upper limit to the students' performance. The student can get each question perfectly right, and he has no possible way of showing that he can do more. With the kind of work usually set, it is normal enough for many students in the class to get ten out of ten, and no one can possibly get eleven. This situation can be improved if some questions in a different style are introduced; and at the same time a much more realistic picture is given of the nature of mathematics in the world outside. Questions can be investigational in nature, with more than one answer, and more than one approach. Questions can be designed to encourage divergent thinking and creativity. It was the aim of some of the projects of the 'sixties to introduce more questions of this type into teaching, although outstanding teachers of the subject have, of course, always used them. But as project material is more and more widely taken up, the intentions of the writers are less and less realised.

Some recent trends in mathematical education may have reduced the incentive to perform numerical calculation. It has been wisely argued that the ability to calculate is of little value unless it is accompanied with understanding—understanding of how to apply the knowledge and how to modify the rules when the circumstances are different. This has led to a mistaken antithesis—do we want ability to calculate *or* do we want understanding? The child who is gifted mathematically undoubtedly wants the opportunity to cultivate both. Some current syllabuses give rather too little encouragement to the able to exercise their calculating skills on a widening range of suitable problems.

Today, all mathematics teachers need to come to terms with the pocket calculator, and to plan carefully so as to give calculators a proper position in mathematics courses. The development of arithmetic in schools in such a way that the majority of children acquire the understanding they need to live in a technical society, plus the facility with numbers to meet everyday needs and to check when calculators have been misused or have gone wrong, presents problems which have still to be solved. For the able child, we need to go beyond this to the development of work schemes and classroom organisation within which he can use calculators to pursue number knowledge extensively for its own sake. This is indeed a challenge.

The further number knowledge which it is appropriate for the able child to investigate (with or without calculators) is by no means the same thing as doing harder sums. When an able child has shown that he can perform reasonable calculations adequately, there is very little to be gained merely by making the arithmetic harder—in the sense of 'more awkward'. The next steps require a genuine knowledge of mathematics on the part of the teacher. If the child's extra number work is to lead on to mathematics then it needs to be carefully structured so that it stimulates conjectures and enables advances to be made by inductive guess-work, which is later validated by deeper reasoning. The able pupil can be encouraged to embark on elementary number theory because he has all the raw material readily to hand.

This presents some difficulties to the teacher who does not possess the knowledge himself. Many books of number puzzles provide useful starting points. These are widely available. Every school should have such books on the classroom shelves, and the local authority library services should be able to give further help if it is required.

Whatever type of school or teaching pattern we are concerned with, the biggest single step forward in the provision for gifted mathematicians would be almost certainly the more effective use of books for individual reading. Many excellent, eminently suitable short books can be bought at very modest prices. In a number of cases publishers market them in an easily identifiable series. Such books are often to be found in school libraries already, but they are hardly ever properly used—and very frequently they are not used at all.

The encouragement of individual reading is part of the larger problem of encouraging various forms of individuality, and of cultivating a climate in which there is collective pride in outstanding achievement by individuals. There is much to be gained from children having the opportunity to teach one another. Arranging for some of the work to be done in groups is one way of bringing this about. Some schools keep a file of especially good solutions to difficult problems, and it becomes an honour to have something put in the file. (One school even tells of the boy whose exercise books were 'confiscated' when he left because his solutions were better than any the staff could produce.)

There are other more fundamental strategies for accommodating gifted pupils. One strategy is to provide accelerated courses. It was more common in the past than it is now for secondary schools to provide a course to O-level mathematics taking only four years instead of the customary five, and there are arguments both ways. Acceleration may be organised for a stream of pupils, or for pupils individually. In the independent sector, pupils are very often speeded through courses according to their level of attainment, rather than by reference to their chronological age, and in this way some mathematicians are years ahead of their fellows. The able 13-year-old can be ready to take O-level, and some pupils have studied on their own to take A-level while their fellows were still preparing for Ordinary. There are also cases in this country of schools making arrangements for an unusually precocious pupil to study for a university degree. Some of these measures are simple matters within the discretion of the school, others may involve further administrative decisions. The arguments for and against acceleration require careful consideration. It is a controversial matter and much depends on the organisational pattern and social climate of the school, as well as on the personality of the individual pupil.

When provision is made for gifted pupils by intensifying the amount of set work covered in the classroom or by homework, it is sometimes a problem for the teacher to decide whether to push on more rapidly with the main line of the course, or whether to branch out and explore the topics being studied by other pupils in greater breadth. This problem is more difficult in middle schools because the pupils subsequently transfer elsewhere. Where there is doubt, it is preferable to choose greater breadth because of the risk of boredom if work is repeated later.

There are less drastic forms of acceleration and many schools provide extra enrichment for the pupils' mathematical studies by some form of supplementary tuition or by club activities outside lesson time. Mathematics clubs can, of course, be open to all pupils who wish to participate, irrespective of their ability. In the experience of HMI, in almost all cases where the mathematical attainments in a school are unusually high, there is some form of voluntary activity outside normal lesson hours. This may range from expeditions by a small group of enthusiasts to a nearby technical college to use the computer, to extra lessons which are specifically directed towards examination objectives. But the effect of further voluntary effort on the everyday work of the classroom can be far beyond anything one might reasonably expect.

Computer activities have often produced a surprising variety and individuality in the work in a school. Whether the school has its own terminal or whether an individual cycles along to the university where he knows the staff, there is something in the activity which fosters initiative and many young mathematicians reveal their talent as a result. Not least of the benefits arising from computer activities in schools are the working relationships established with mathematicians outside.

A sub-committee of the Mathematical Association organises national competitions in mathematics, and arranges participation in the International Olympiad. English achievement in these competitions compares favourably with other countries', but over the years it is consistently plain that the high achieving pupils come disproportionately from high prestige schools. The same must be said about scholarship awards to the older universities. There is evidence to suggest that nature distributes mathematical potential with much less regard for parents' occupational grouping. If between the ages of 11 and 18 the potentially good mathematician is not accelerated, all is not lost, but it should be a matter for public concern that opportunities for acceleration are so inequitably distributed.

It is distasteful to some to stress the competitive aspects of mathematics; but there are collaborative aspects also, and these could be more intensively cultivated. School pupils have written mathematical articles which have been published in a variety of journals, and more than one school has published its own mathematical magazine. In some cases the students' writing has been of a very high standard. Mathematical lines of enquiry could be more effectively pursued in science fairs and similar activities.

Opportunities for gifted pupils are frequently provided by LEAs, colleges and universities. These vary in nature from short residential courses to series of evening lectures and the students can be involved in a variety of ways. In some areas, local branches of the Mathematical Association organise meetings directed to sixth formers as well as to teachers. It is always better if there can be some element of continuity and follow-up in these activities, and in undertaking this LEAs are in an advantageous position. At least one LEA arranges courses in conjunction with the local university.

Let us leave the last word to a child who had been on a two-day 'workshop' course, organised by the LEA for children from middle schools showing exceptional promise in mathematics:

> '. . . a thing I feel quite strongly about and that is in some way to tell us or make it possible for us to find out for ourselves how certain formulae or tables are established; i.e. we know what πr^2, πd and $\pi r^2 h$ equal, but how do we get them? How do we know that π equals 3·14 or 22/7, or even Pythagoras' Theorem equals what it does? How do they decide upon logarithm tables? I think that this point should be taken up because it is a useful thing to know this information.'*

* Quoted in *Trends in Education*, 1977/2.

This point should indeed be taken up. In too many cases schools do not provide for such appetites to be fed.

8   Modern Languages

**What is a gifted
modern linguist?**

The difficulty of responding to this question reflects differing views
of the value of language competence. If a child is bilingual, speaking
fluently and idiomatically at one moment as a Frenchman and at the
next as a German, he might be called gifted by some, but ordinary
by those who by chance were born in a geographical area where the
dual use of language is customary. Or again, is the individual who
has mastered one foreign language more gifted than one who has
some familiarity with ten languages? The demonstration of giftedness is less absolute than in many curriculum areas, and in conse-
quence presents greater difficulty of definition.

In the school context, teachers are rarely concerned with teaching
a multiplicity of languages, nor with the total mastery of languages
which characterises a Council of Europe interpreter. Giftedness in
the school context is applied to facility in acquiring distinct skills in
language without the advantage of living in a community where the
language is the daily medium of communication. It is commonly
agreed that these skills are:

> understanding the foreign language when spoken by a native
> speaker at the normal speed of conversation;
> speaking the language fully intelligibly to the native speaker at the
> normal speed of conversation;
> reading the language with ease:
> writing the language correctly in expressing his own thoughts.

The difficulty of definition derives from the differences in the
nature of these four skills. It seems likely that there are gifted performers with a high degree of mimetic ability who can learn to
understand and speak foreign languages with impressive facility,
while showing at best only moderate skill in reading and writing
them. There appear to be others for whom the reverse is true: their
command of the written word, in reading or writing, greatly exceeds
their oral ability. It may be that oral skills demand a particular,
specific ability, whereas proficiency in reading and writing can be
regarded as a function of general intellectual ability. If that is true,
it follows that in schools, where considerable importance is attached
to reading and writing in language-learning, as indeed the form of
external examinations demands that it should be, giftedness in
modern languages will almost invariably be found only in pupils
who combine specific talents with a high general ability and will, if
circumstances are propitious, manifest itself in outstanding academic
performance. The pupil with ability in modern languages is likely
to do careful work. The gifted pupil is likely to do work which is
careful, but which also shows signs of a fellow-feeling for the
language. To some extent, the gifted pupil 'becomes' French while
using the language, whereas the merely able pupil uses French
efficiently, but without identifying with it.

In the study of literature, the gifted linguist shows insight and fellow-feeling in the use of individual words and the organisation of word patterns to a marked extent. There are examples of authors who have acquired sufficient command of a second language to be accepted by the second culture as a contributor to it. Conrad, Nabokov, Chamisso and Koestler have not only acquired a foreign language but empathised with it to the point of metamorphosis into the very 'foreigner' whom they began by merely imitating. These are the rarest exceptions; but the empathy which they have in common is a characteristic of giftedness in modern language, even at the more modest level of school.

In addition to the difficulty of definition, there are few ways of identification of potential giftedness prior to actual performance. In this sense, provision has to precede identification.

Modern language provision at the present time

In terms of both identification of and provision for gifted linguists, informed observers find considerable cause for concern in the present state of modern languages in schools. *Trends in Education* (1976/1) contains two articles devoted to the teaching of foreign languages, and in the editorial comment, 'Talking Points', it is stated: 'Professor Hawkins notes that fewer of the most able are achieving examination success and that the numbers of modern language entrants for both O- and A-level examinations are falling. Other observers believe that the top 20 per cent of pupils who constitute our traditional language learners are today achieving less than their potential. There are significantly more places available for modern languages in universities than there are suitable candidates to fill them. Mr Williams (Staff Inspector, DES) ruefully concludes that this country produces "only a small number of competent linguists and that efforts to give substantial numbers worthwhile knowledge of a foreign language have met with little success".'

Concern is also frequently expressed about the possible effects of mixed ability grouping upon performance in modern languages. This form of organisation, increasingly popular in the early years of secondary education, finds its theoretical justification in the possibility which it offers of providing for individual needs, but it has in fact proved extraordinarily difficult to arrange effective individual assignments for beginners in modern languages, who have little knowledge and few skills on which such work can be based and for whom, as has been said, the teacher remains the sole source of authority. Consequently, all too often the group is taught as a class, with the level pitched somewhere around the middle, so that the needs of the most (as of the least) able are neglected and the work proceeds at a very slow pace.

Other problems which have to be faced concern the effects of sex and class differences upon performance in modern languages. In his article in *Trends in Education* (1976/1), Professor Hawkins cites convincing evidence to show that 'serious linguists', as he calls them, are mostly girls and mostly middle class. The former finding, which is confirmed by HMI observation, is supported by Certificate of Secondary Education and General Certificate of Education O- and A-level results, which point clearly to the superiority of girls—and the disparity is increasing year by year. Mixed schools appear to have a depressive effect upon boys' motivation and performance in modern languages; there is evidence to suggest that boys do better in segregated schools or groups. Support for the thesis that middle class children are more successful than others in language learning comes mainly from Dr Clare Burstall's report, *French in the Primary School,* which shows that there is 'a linear relationship between test score and parental occupation', and that middle class families generally support modern language study. This view receives some confirmation from the head of modern languages at the comprehensive school studied in *The Creighton Report* (Hunter Davies), who is quoted as saying: 'I think England's social system has a bad effect on foreign languages. A working class boy, as I was, doesn't get the enormous home encouragement of the middle classes. Boys particularly seem less amenable to foreign languages'. If these assertions are justified, gifted working class boys in mixed schools must be considered as peculiarly at risk so far as the realisation of their potential in modern languages is concerned.

Teaching methods have an obvious influence upon pupils' performance. The general adoption of audio-visual courses in modern languages (though they are not always used as they were meant to be) has led to a notable improvement in standards of listening comprehension and, to some extent, of oral production, but in some cases they have impeded the able linguist's rapid analysis and assimilation of language structures. Furthermore, in many schools inadequate attention is accorded to the skills of writing and reading—particularly rapid silent reading, which is essential for the development of the gifted linguist.

Very few comprehensive schools appear to make special provision for the linguistically gifted pupil by any form of acceleration or enrichment. One school, which is situated in a favourable area and is anxious to achieve good academic standards, takes advantage of the fact that most of its incoming pupils have studied French in the primary school and enters the top set for O-level French in the fourth year; in that way it makes more time available for the study of German which is undertaken as a two-year course begun in the fourth year. However, that form of organisational arrangement is unlikely to occur very often. One interesting experiment is the creation in three English schools (one an independent school and another a selective school) of 'sections bilingues'—bilingual classes in which the foreign language is used for the teaching of subjects such as history and geography. The experiment offers good prospects of success provided that the pupils and the teachers taking part in it can be selected with the utmost care.

Entry into the European Economic Community underlines the desirability of equipping far more of our professional people with a command of foreign languages extending beyond a pass at O-level, but sixth form courses for non-specialists seem to occupy a very low place in the order of priorities of most schools.

The picture of support by outside agencies is obscure. It is not common for local education authorities to make special arrangements for gifted children in modern languages, but a few have organised short intensive residential courses for able school pupils with a special interest in languages. In one authority which is fortunate in having two excellent and attractive residential centres, the modern languages adviser, assisted by the full-time director of the language centre, has offered a number of intensive courses which have proved very popular and successful. In one of these, the main aims were said to be 'to boost motivation and to improve language facility and O-level skills', and the organiser reports: 'The linguistic progress of the pupils was remarkable in pronunciation, comprehension, confidence, fluency and accuracy. From a sticky start on Friday evening, progress was made to uninhibited and animated discussions on Sunday afternoon with most of the pupils'. Another authority organised a two-day series of lectures for some twenty linguistically able sixth formers, and in his report, the organiser says: 'My conclusions are that such conferences and gatherings provide an invaluable and unique experience for minority subjects such as languages at sixth form level . . . The use of resource materials to stretch and stimulate some pupils is of use, but the most important thing is the contact of mind with mind'. Some authorities have also been enterprising in arranging and helping to finance exchange and other study visits to foreign countries, and it is to be hoped that financial constraints will not make it impossible to continue such initiatives.

Conclusions

It is difficult to avoid the conclusion that modern languages face serious problems in many comprehensive schools at present.

One of the major impediments to the development of effective modern language teaching is the persistent shortage of appropriately qualified specialist staff. This is itself a product of secondary re-organisation, which has greatly increased the number of schools aspiring to teach at least one foreign language and has, moreover, made further demands upon staffing by the almost universal tendency to extend the teaching of the first foreign language to the whole ability range, in the early years at least. Both these outcomes are entirely commendable in that they reflect the desire to extend to all the advantages formerly enjoyed only by a few, but when resources are strictly limited, a more equal distribution may mean that the most able suffer by comparison with the past. Despite an expansion during the last decade from one-third to two-thirds of secondary school pupils studying a modern language, teachers note with concern a high drop-out rate in the middle years before pupils achieve anything worthwhile.

There is still a significant number of schools in which the provision even of only one foreign language at an appropriate level presents severe difficulties and in which, therefore, the gifted linguist is likely to find himself at a serious disadvantage. The position of the second foreign language is, understandably, even more critical on logistical grounds alone, without taking into account the reluctance of some heads—fewer now than formerly, perhaps—to offer a subject which might be thought divisive in that it is likely to be studied with profit only by those who have given proof of linguistic ability. It is rare to find a comprehensive school in which a pupil would be permitted to study more than two foreign languages.

9   Music

Identification of the gifted musician

Traditionally, musically gifted children have been identified through formal or informal auditions. Such measurement has important limitations since it assesses attainment rather than potential and may therefore give greater weight to acquired skills than to innate gifts; hence, these skills may become an end in themselves and the time spent in gaining them may be at the expense of other interests. To remedy this, tests have been devised which may help to identify musical potential more accurately.

More emphasis is now being given to less teachable elements (for example an acute ear and a flair for improvisation) than to those more likely to be the results of good tuition. It must be recognised, though, that a child with no aural training may not easily demonstrate acuteness of ear, and a child with limited skill as an instrumentalist may have difficulty in expressing genuine inventiveness when asked to improvise. It may not be easy to distinguish between innate gifts and acquired skills, but they can be assessed qualitively, if not precisely, and sensed subjectively on a scale progressing from competency to those endowed with exceptional gifts; these pupils are likely to possess an instinctive sense of style, an understanding of what music is about, and a natural physical and intellectual rapport with their chosen instrument.

The vital need for support at an early age

An understanding of this is helpful because of the importance which musicians attach to the need for musical skills and interests to be encouraged at an early age if gifted children are to emerge. In practice, this has usually meant beginning instrumental lessons, often keyboard or strings, between the ages of 5 and 10. This, in turn, has depended for success on the supportive role of the family and the chance circumstances which may bring together fruitfully the child, the teacher and the right choice of instrument. There may be a number of children whose innate musical ability is considerable though it remains undeveloped because geographical and social factors are unfavourable. On the other hand, the development of a prodigious instrumental technique in young children may not, of itself, indicate an outstanding musical gift nor presage a willing commitment to music later. With many children, a lasting commitment seems to occur in early adolescence. The importance of informed and accurate advice to young musicians and their parents, based on probing, expert and continuous assessment, needs to be emphasised. Parents must know that early competence and enthusiasm may not always continue in later years. That said, the stimulus and encouragement which the home may provide in the early years and after schooling begins appear to be crucial in providing the environment in which, with appropriate teaching, musical talent and potential may materialise. By appropriate teaching is implied a consistent course which fosters a steady, dedicated and

Provision for gifted musicians

disciplined approach to music probably before the age at which secondary schooling begins.

Until recent years, opportunities for individual musical experience among younger children were left largely to the initiative of parents (with a small and diminishing role for the church choir or local band) while schools and education authorities concentrated most of their resources in secondary schools where many of the more highly trained music teachers are available to organise and direct such teaching. As the disadvantage of starting string teaching after the age of 11 have become apparent much effort has gone into beginning this, and other instrumental teaching, at a younger age—in the first or second year of the junior or middle school and sometimes earlier. The sheer logistics of containing the consequent increase in children wishing to participate has led authorities to organise music centres, usually held on Saturdays, but sometimes on weekday evenings as well. More economic provision can thus be made and extra resources and better organisation can attempt to meet the needs of a small number of potentially more able pupils whom such arrangements may identify. Some authorities now have fairly elaborate and detailed schemes for the musical development of some children through group and individual tuition in schools and music centres; through the provision of grants for more advanced work with tutors elsewhere; and by the award of junior exhibition places at colleges of music, where they exist.

There have been, in addition, two other developments during the last decade. There is now a small number of independent music schools most of whose pupils are assisted in part or in full by grants from LEAs or through foundations such as Gulbenkian or Leverhulme. These schools, widely differing in character and organisation and usually spanning the primary and secondary age range, account for several hundred highly gifted young musicians and have become an established part of the musical and educational life of the country. The other development, initially seen as meeting some of the needs indicated by the demand for independent music school places, has been the setting up within a normal comprehensive school of a special musically biased course designed to attract an annual half form entry chosen by audition. There is one example of this now in its sixth year of operation with about 90 auditioned musicians among 1600 other pupils; other authorities do not seem inclined to set up similar arrangements.

The strength of the specialist music schools lies in their bringing together on a continuous basis a number of gifted musicians with complementary talents and enthusiasms, and in their organisation of the curriculum itself, with musical studies as the central core, surrounded by a range of alternative studies up to O- and A-level. Thus pupils can spend up to two hours or more daily in their individual musical studies, participate in a wide range of ensemble work with other gifted musicians, and undertake supervised practice as part of the course structure independent of individual home circumstances. With so few specialist music schools in this country it is inevitable that, for a number of pupils, such opportunities can be met only through a boarding place, one of the factors which contributes to the high costs in such schools. The contrast with the expense of a place in a maintained middle or comprehensive school is obvious, but a fairer comparison might be with a boarding place in other forms of special education.

Although over half the local education authorities have supported pupils in these music schools at some period, it is an opportunity which is limited to a small proportion of musically gifted children, the majority of whom are bound to depend on local resources in their schools and within the LEA.

Limitations on provision for gifted musicians

There are considerable difficulties in making such resources equally available for these children from school to school and from one LEA to another. The most obvious limitation is that of distribution. Most musicians congregate in the conurbations which house the institutions and organisations providing employment—broadcasting studios, the colleges and departments of music, the principal orchestras and performance ensembles. This provides a part-time teaching force with a strong element of current professional experience and encourages the general growth of music making and teaching at a professional level throughout the area. Far less well off are the more sparsely populated, sometimes rural, areas which may lack not only indigenous musical resources but which, with smaller schools and difficulties of travel, find it hard to provide even a restricted peripatetic teaching service. These limitations restrict the opportunities for musical children of all abilities; for the gifted, for whom there could be an overriding need to work (for a time) with one particular teacher, they can be quite disastrous.

The importance of the home and family in providing worthwhile musical experience and encouragement at an early and impressionable age has already been touched upon. Many gifted musicians have emerged for whom this kind of support, either within the immediate family circle, or through a close relationship with a gifted teacher early on, has been a key influence in triggering off the interest and commitment which develops into artistry and the fostering of individual musical gifts. For pupils whose musical interests and gifts are discerned in later years, often in the secondary school, there are opportunities of musical fulfilment—but their breadth and range is likely to be curtailed and the lack of early musical experience may remain a handicap, whether in a technical/instrumental sense, or in the fullest development of an 'inner ear'. For such older pupils, the most likely aims could be music as a vocal study, or in composition, history or criticism, or in teaching and the direction of music, all areas where maturity and experience are an advantage.

In view of the number of ways in which musical potential can develop, LEAs have shown much resourcefulness in providing options within which children with musical gifts may be helped and encouraged. But some traditional ideas no longer reflect current needs and should be reconsidered.

A primary concern must be the narrowly conceived nature of much of the musical curriculum. Many authorities concentrate most, if not all, their specialist resources on those instrumental techniques which provide the basis for the orchestra of the late nineteenth century. Even when slightly more contemporary idioms or skills are encouraged, it is almost always to meet the demands of classical orchestral studies. While such studies may be a considerable and proper part of any provision, this does underestimate and under-value the importance of keyboard skills, still perhaps the most use-ful general musical competence needed by any musician. It also fails to appreciate and encourage the development of talent in other areas of musical experience, those based in different social, ethnic and cultural traditions. In so doing, music is set apart as a European study in history and performance. The need for experiment and innovation is urgent, and an exploratory, expressive and venture-some approach deserves some share of any resources set aside for musical education.

Another constraint has been the extent to which instrumental activities have been accepted as a normal part of the curriculum. When they do not fall in this category, the cost usually falls on indi-vidual pupils, with the schools helping where they can, but the burdens can become intolerable. There are other inequalities, for example where instrumental teaching is available only in a 'group' situation regardless of need, where arrangements for the loan, hire or purchase of instruments fail to mitigate the wide disparity of costs, or where insufficient account has been taken of differing levels of parental support.

The general effect of anomalies of this nature is to penalise the studies of those pupils who show the greatest promise and achieve some distinction. As more gifted musicians are encouraged to broaden their studies they may encounter a growing burden, for example an advanced string player may require theoretical and keyboard studies to provide the balanced scholarship with which to support a principal study on a solo instrument. It is in these areas that apparently reasonable decisions taken to meet the needs of the majority of pupils can adversely affect the very small numbers of exceptional children whose musical needs probably require individual assessment and provision.

Conclusions

However, in some middle and comprehensive schools, children gifted in music are being identified, their needs diagnosed and a suitable course of activity made available in one or other of the ways already indicated. The problems in music are perhaps different from other subjects in that the search for the gifted musician has always been a prime concern, sometimes at the expense of more mundane, but no less worthwhile, aims. If better use is to be made of the resources which already exist for the education of musically gifted children, the following are some of the questions which ought to be con-sidered:

i. Whether a more systematic means of identifying potentially gifted musicians at an early age might make it easier to assess pupils' needs more accurately in the middle or later secondary years.

ii. Whether a better definition of 'pupils with outstanding musical gifts' might make it possible to provide a more flexible and indi-vidual response to their needs without necessarily incurring greater costs. In this way some of the possible inequalities of circumstance and location may be avoided.

iii. Whether useful distinctions can be drawn between those pupils for whom a continuous course of study with music as the centre of the curriculum is essential and others, perhaps of equal gifts, for whom schooling in the normal way, together with additional peripheral opportunities, is equally suitable.

iv. Whether there is a place for a musically biased course designed to attract an entry of gifted musicians by audition and based on an existing or intended comprehensive school? Could such a course meet the needs of pupils for whom a place at an independent music school is not possible but for whom other arrangements might otherwise be inadequate? And is 11 the right age for such a course to begin while other experience suggests a probable age of 8?

These are the questions which might be asked in any assessment of the way in which gifted children in music fare in middle and comprehensive schools in one part of the country or another. The answers may not support the need for more resources or more expenditure, so much as the better use of existing provision.

Recognition of the physically gifted

The first concern of physical education in the school curriculum lies with recognising the individuality of human movement and therefore offering many opportunities for self realisation through this medium. A balanced programme therefore includes different forms of activity. The achievement of a high level of performance in a particular activity is an outcome for some of this initial experience. Giftedness in movement is discernible in the expressive forms of dance and drama just as clearly as in the execution of specific objective skills such as gymnastics, swimming and other forms of sport which depend on competitive procedures.

The identification of the physically gifted is dependent on many factors. Of prime importance is the opportunity to take part in the chosen activity. In the past much talent has remained undeveloped. With the widening opportunities for participation in physical activities at school and elsewhere, together with the growth of facilities and the development of coaching schemes, less is left to chance today. But chance will continue to play a considerable part. The choice of leisure pursuits and the levels at which they are practised will always reflect influences felt and opportunities presented at certain times critical to the individual. Paramount in the identification of the potentially gifted will be the general development of opportunities for all so that talent, where it exists, will emerge and the element of chance will be reduced.

Gifted achievement in physical performance is easy to recognise. Excellence of execution is there for even the layman to see but gifted potential in physical activity is beset with problems of recognition. The diversity of physical activity makes generalisation difficult; the qualities of a good fencer, good games player, dancer, sailor, swimmer, gymnast or rock climber may show quite different groupings of characteristics. Experienced physical education teachers can readily identify individual attributes of strength, endurance, agility and coordination. They may also note interest, determination, the capacity to improve through practice or skilled teaching. Yet without the observation of actual performance in a sport or other physical activity, it is virtually impossible from a consideration of general physical attributes to identify potential giftedness in specific areas.

Provision for the physically gifted

Schools are one of the most influential of the many agencies which endeavour to ensure that opportunities are available for participation in physical activities. Teachers will be concerned with the physical education of all pupils. They will also be anxious to recognise talent above the ordinary and will seek ways of developing it which constraints of the normal programme may not allow. It may be thought that those who show themselves to be exceptionally able in athletic pursuits would have unrivalled opportunities in large comprehensive schools with good facilities and well staffed physical education departments. This is not necessarily so. It is possible that among the large numbers involved and in the complexities of the organisation some gifted performers may not emerge. The programme may be too diverse or the experiences provided may be too superficial. Some gifted children may achieve recognition only in the smaller institutions. Physical education departments must try to provide programmes for a full range of abilities. Satisfaction in the achievement of success in physical activities is as necessary for the low level performer as for the high.

The presence in a school of a dedicated and committed enthusiast prepared to give freely of his own time for coaching purposes is often the important factor in the development of the talent of the gifted performer. He may or may not be a physical educationist or an outstanding performer himself, but his well-developed knowledge and enthusiasm will guide children towards increasingly high levels in their chosen sport. For example, a pupil in a comprehensive school in the north of England owes his present situation as a contender for a place in the British fencing team to the help and encouragement of his art teacher.

Most team games and the most popular individual sports are supported by a comprehensive structure of school associations in addition to school based competitions. These are usually administered by teachers in a voluntary capacity and offer competition at district, county and national representative levels, providing opportunities for the gifted performer to compete alongside the best exponents of his chosen sport.

Other opportunities for the exceptionally able are provided by agencies outside the school. Many schools make contact with clubs in their vicinity where arrangements have been made for young people to join the junior section and perhaps to receive coaching by experts. Some local education authorities provide holiday coaching schemes; others provide special centres including residential centres with opportunities for specialist training in adventure pursuits. In general, LEA advisers are anxious to identify emerging excellence and to ensure some form of 'enriching' provision. For example, one London borough has a number of 'centres for special interest' in ten different activities, including dance, where regular coaching is provided for promising and interested young performers from the borough's schools and from the community at large. Each centre is at a school which is equipped appropriately for the activity and where qualified coaching staff are employed. Most of the staff are peripatetic instructors who are employed by day in the borough's schools, where they have identified the promising performer and invited him to attend the centre in the evening. Two boys for whom the scheme has worked well are:

i. David, who first took part in curriculum judo at the age of 12, was identified quickly as a potentially gifted performer. He was invited to attend the special interest class for judo by his judo teacher. By the age of 17 he was attending judo classes four or five times a week. At 23 he is now an international competitor and was a reserve for the British Judo team at the Montreal Olympic Games.

ii. Robin, aged 14, began to take part in fencing at the age of 9, encouraged by his father who had been a fencer. He joined the special class for fencing before he left his junior school. He now attends a secondary comprehensive school and continues to be a member of his special interest class. He was identified as gifted by the fencing professor and received extra tuition from him. He has been county under-14 fencing champion for the last three seasons and is now being considered for training with the British under-20 team. He trains four evenings a week. It is interesting to note that the cost to his parents is estimated at over £100 a year in spite of virtually free tuition.

A county local education authority pays the salaries of five well qualified coaches who administer schemes for the coaching of the exceptionally gifted performers in gymnastics, trampolining, tennis, badminton and cycling. Part of the salary of a swimming coach is also provided. Except for swimming, the coaching takes place in local authority schools where facilities are appropriate and for which no charge is made. The principles for each scheme are to unite the performers in a club structure with additional voluntary coaches and to give them opportunities for individual and team competitions of the highest order. In another example, a local authority in a provincial town provides coaching for swimmers who have been identified and selected following successful participation in inter-school competition. A number of those involved have reached the highest levels of international competition.

Other agencies which provide opportunities for gifted sportsmen, and which are in receipt of government funds, are the national governing bodies of sport. Projected regional and national 'centres of excellence' where the outstanding sportsmen and sportswomen can meet for special coaching are developing. Certain commercial concerns have for many years sponsored a number of sports and provided funds for residential courses and for competitions. Clubs and courses are also run at a number of municipal recreation centres and children from 8 years of age and upwards are being introduced to such activities as judo and Olympic gymnastics. In this latter case it is too early to assess the effects that this will have on the future development of talent but it should result in higher levels of performance nationally, provided that enthusiasm can be matched by technically competent and sensitive coaching.

In the majority of sports, talented performers are heavily involved with their sport from an early age and are committed to demanding training schedules for their chosen activity long before they leave school. With rare exceptions, the training takes place outside school hours. For example, Kate, now aged 16, was introduced by her parents to a junior badminton club while still at her junior school. Though she has never played badminton at her junior or secondary comprehensive school, she has represented her county, is in the national youth 'squad' and has travelled abroad for international competition. She plays badminton for 15 hours a week on weekday evenings and spends most weekends taking part in tournaments.

The cost to Kate's parents is approximately £400 a year. Television recently featured a 13-year-old girl swimmer who pursued a course of training which demanded that she wake before 4 a.m. on three mornings a week to travel to the pool at which her coach operated and to return home before going to school.

Just as there are those gifted in competitive sports, there are those with gifts for expressive forms of physical activity. Various opportunities exist for the development of such talent within and outside schools. Small groups studying dance intensively for examination purposes have enabled their members to develop the resources essential for skilled performance. Festivals and days of dance enrich the experience of children by the interaction of pupils from several schools. Professional schools of dance provide opportunities for pursuing the technical training essential to the dancer and financial support is available. One large comprehensive school admits both boys and girls from other areas to attend regular classes at a local dancing school. Seminars are held regularly in the north of England for school children from a wide area to pursue their training in a residential setting. For the child in the middle or comprehensive school, recognition of this form of giftedness may be of greater and more lasting significance than the more ephemeral eye-catching aspects of competitive activities.

Conclusion

The impracticability of a national scheme for screening early physical talent is evident. It would be costly in effort and time and unreliable in its diagnosis. Although there are more opportunities today than in the past, it is inevitable that chance will continue to play its part in the individual choice of physical activities. The physically gifted stand a good chance of being identified in schools which offer an adequate range of expertise and resources. Beyond recognition and early training, schools realise the limitations on their ability to provide time, specialised coaching and suitable competition. Physical education teachers rightly see their task as the all-round physical development of all children and are cautious about the effects of the excessive pursuit of excellence for the few.

It is important to distinguish between success which is the result only of early maturation and true physical giftedness. Over concentration on those who develop early may cause the talent of those who develop more slowly to be overlooked. The presence of highly gifted performers may be an incentive to others and may serve to raise general levels of performance. However, in some cases, their presence may act as a deterrent to those who do not excel.

There are strong pressures in our society for competitive sport in school. Many pupils who become good gymnasts, swimmers or footballers acquire prestige in the eyes of their fellows. Parents often would wish their children to become successful sportsmen and schools to provide outlets in competitive sports. Teachers may seek fulfilment in the success of their pupils. High level competition means a heavy commitment of their time for the participants. For example, swimming or gymnastics can involve the performer in practical training far in excess of 16 hours each week. Without the loyal support of parents many children would be unable to compete at this level.

The effects of these early and prolonged pressures on the lives of young people and their families need to be examined critically. Parents and teachers must consider carefully before setting in motion a course of action which demands such sacrifice and single-mindedness of them and their charges. They will need to be re-assured on certain important issues. Are the emotional strains of international competition too great for those of tender years? Is the time commitment to a single activity excessive for young people and are they spending their time as profitably as they might if they were following a broader range of interests? For those who do not achieve success at the highest level after years of preparation, what will be the effects of disappointment and rejection? Where there are competitions there are many more losers than winners. Where the choice is made, however, the majority of schools point the highly gifted in the direction of extra-curricular provision both inside and outside the school.

11 Science

Recognition of giftedness in science

HMIs regard the following characteristics as indicators of giftedness in science pupils:

> Seeing the relevance of what is learned in a science lesson to situations outside the laboratory.
> Capacity to leap ahead or to jump steps in an argument and to detect faulty logic.
> Desire to quantify experimental results by counting, weighing or otherwise measuring.
> Dissatisfaction with over-generalised explanation and inadequate detail.
> Rapid perception of the direction of an investigation and anticipation of realistic outcomes.
> Connection of scattered or disparate data into coherent patterns.
> Persistent pursuit of an investigation until all reasonable avenues have been explored.
> Ability to hold a problem in the mind and analyse it; in other words good powers of concentration.

Some of these characteristics can be illustrated by examples encountered during school visits:

Peggy, a third former, with a fast, clear mind. She thought that some of the Nuffield type experimental work was too 'obvious' and knew the result before the experiment was over. Moreover, she thought that the class experimental results were often 'poor and variable' and that 'more straightforward experiments should be given to get through the basics rapidly, and that more project work should be done to really find out'. She could get the better of her teachers and appeared arrogant.

Tony, aged 13, was very single-minded. His only interest was in physics and chemistry. He knew a great deal of physics, and his bible was Nelkon's O-level physics. In his work he said he tried to go 'deeply into experiments'.

Pradip, an Indian boy, aged 13, was articulate and clear-minded. He explained the snags in arguing about the natural behaviour of woodlice from an experiment he had set up in the laboratory. He saw too, without prompting, that the laboratory observations needed to be checked by field observations in natural conditions.

John, aged 14, articulate, clear-headed, with a quick and accurate grasp of the physics he was doing; he was also widely read. He found *1984* so depressing that he gave it up: 'It was too real.'

Peter, an upper sixth former, had a reflective rather than a fast logical mind. He had a great deal of imagination and width of interest. He said that physicists (he wanted to study physics at the university) were used to altering only one variable in an experiment, keeping the rest constant and, by doing so, may oversimplify 'compared with biologists who were used to handling complex data'. 'That is why Crick and Watson broke the DNA code in six weeks, two different minds bent on the same problem.'

All the pupils described above were picked out by teachers; some had an IQ below 130. In fact, although an above average IQ appears to be essential in progress towards eminence in science, exceptional intelligence is not necessarily a prerequisite. For example, in a top science set in an 11–16 comprehensive school:

'The set responded to a number of questions which demanded that the class devise hypotheses and experiments to test them. The pupils giving the best response proved to be pupils with an IQ of 108–115 rather than those with an IQ over 130. The latter seemed content to listen and to write very neat correct notes.'

The complexity of recognition of scientific giftedness is clear; there is not one type of giftedness in science but a mixture of characteristics, some cognitive, others of personality which combine in differing proportions: of these, logic, imagination and persistence are qualities that seem necessary for eventual high achievement in science, but not necessarily a high IQ. In a rough and ready sense, there may be two types of giftedness in science observed in their early stages in the characteristics and work of the children seen: 'masters of their subject', or those who know the major concepts and skills of a discipline; and 'puzzlers', or those who find, by 'thinking aloud' or concentrating on a problem for days or weeks, that conventional formulae conceal gaps and unjustified assumptions that have been 'avoided by a plausible but ambiguous turn of phrase or an implicit but illegitimate assumption'.*

What is done for children gifted in science

This can be summed up in a sentence: science teachers are generally aware of the gifted, but have few solutions about how to provide for them. As far as organisational patterns for grouping children are concerned, all contain weaknesses. Observation suggests that banding and setting helps science teachers to some extent to identify gifted pupils and sustain a general high level of demand and stimulus, but these pupils seldom get individual attention. In banding and setting, there is also the danger of some pupils being misplaced in terms of potential ability so that teacher expectation operates in the wrong way. Mixed ability grouping (as illustrated below in HMI observation of a class) makes considerable demands upon teacher time and energy:

'We found a combination of circumstances which might be typical of some situations we shall meet and may possibly be a "case history" of great significance and general application: a successful arrangement of mixed ability classes for the first two years with

* Hayek, F.A. 'Types of Mind'. *Encounter*. September 1975.

setting in the third year (for most subjects); a good sprinkling of very able children taught by a team of hardworking, dedicated staff, who are unstinting in the time they give to the school. The staff themselves are not brilliant but pull together as a team. They are well aware of the strength and needs of individual pupils, including those of the very bright: the records they send to the Upper School are outstandingly good, but very little is being done for the very able, and the teachers recognise this. But the hard fact remains that their day is taken up by teaching classes of about 30; some of the very bright or gifted pupils are very demanding. They ask questions, seek comment from the teacher on all their work. There is not enough time given over by the teacher for marking (and therefore diagnosis of needs is weak) and a lot of time is spent in preparation of lessons. Ancillary staff are in short supply. The staff put much effort into club activity. Is there much more that this staff could do for the very able within class time?'

And from the same school, a more specific comment on the science:

'The science staff is hardworking, and academically not well-qualified; they are honest and caring. The very bright children are getting a sound science base, with plenty of experimental work and project work, but little is done for them specially. The staff do their best and worry about maintaining a balance between "specials" and "majority" needs.'

Clearly class size is a major constraint on how far a science teacher can provide differentiated materials and differentiated expectations in a mixed ability organisation. Commercial worksheets and extension materials exist, but for the bright pupil, some worksheets appear to be too cramping; there is perhaps a need for less information on them about how to set up an experiment and occasions need to be made for discussion with the teacher and with the group the gifted pupil is working in so that a young mind is sharpened and made to think deeply.

Some schools attempt the use of the project method as a means of extending more able pupils. In biology, project work seen by HMI included the construction of a hypothesis, its testing by experiment, leading on to further observation and experiments. In the best classes, further ideas for investigation were suggested and the project was sometimes linked with published evidence. Statistical tests were used and interpreted. Most important, even with a negative conclusion, what went wrong was described and experiments were suggested that might have been done.

In the last analysis however, the most important factor for the gifted child is to meet the teacher who can identify his gifts and elicit the appropriate responses. Crucial is the teacher's knowledge of his/her subjects, as well as enthusiasm and level of expectancy. Equally important is the sheer craftsmanship of marking and the teacher's ability to assess progress; plan ahead; be able to put a good book in the hands of a pupil; suggest what he/she thinks about a particular way of tackling an experiment; or send a pupil to see an 'expert' the teacher knows.

One example of a scientifically gifted boy from a comprehensive school in an overspill area of a big city may serve to illustrate several of these aspects of provision.

The boy's father was a lorry driver, his mother worked as a clerk but the parents were separated. The primary school record was not outstanding. On Moray House tests the VR score was 108, the NVR, 114. The secondary school he entered was streamed, and set for mathematics across the streams. As the boy moved through the school he showed himself to be an excellent worker with great persistence. He was one of a group of four who enjoyed competing with one another, particularly in mathematics. He was popular and a good all-rounder. His O-level results in maths and three sciences and engineering drawing were all grade 1 but in language and literature they were grade 4 and 5. In the sixth form, he got four grade As—in maths, further maths, physics and chemistry—and a grade B in general studies. He obtained a grade 1 in scholarship maths but was unclassified in scholarship physics. The teaching he received in the sixth form is interesting. His maths master, a non-graduate in his 'fifties who had also taught him in the fourth and fifth years, said that teaching Colin had been the most stimulating experience he had ever had in teaching. He added that he thought in the last six months he had guided rather than taught the boy. The physicist, a graduate, had also taught Colin in the fourth and fifth years but there had been three changes in the chemistry department while Colin was in the sixth form. The staff feel that this is why he just missed getting into Cambridge. Attempting the examination in his second year in the sixth he was at a disadvantage and the weakness in chemistry didn't help. The historian who took the general studies was highly impressed by his wide reading, in particular his interest in and grasp of economics.

It would be unsound to argue from one isolated incident such as this, but a few points are worth emphasising which are backed by wider observation than this illustration and serve to summarise this section. First, the fair, not brilliant, IQ scores from primary school, persistence even against difficulties in his home background, and qualities mentioned earlier as characteristic of the scientifically gifted. Second, the organisational arrangements which brought him into contact with like minds. Finally, the influence of the staff interaction with the boy, in particular concern and level of expectancy.

Conclusions and suggestions

Science teachers can pick out the characteristics listed in the first section, but it is doubtful if the practice of actually doing this with a view to meeting need is widespread. Gifted children may be overlooked simply because the organisational system, the range of differentiated materials, or the opportunities for enriching activities are deficient. In short, gifted children may go undetected, or detected but unsupported. What can be done? In the first place, some of the science taught needs to be of an investigational nature. Didactic teaching will not call forth a need to devise hypotheses and experiments to test them. Teaching approach and content must give an opportunity for the characteristics listed at the outset to emerge.

Project work is one way of eliciting high level scientific behaviour. But it should not be a teaching method in which able pupils are left without access to suitable resources or to a supportive teacher. Fieldwork expeditions are another way.

Second, a policy of recording characteristics, as well as skills, knowledge and the more evident signs of competence is needed.

Third, whatever organisational structure exists in a school, there will be the need for enriching experiences which extend the gifted. The vital influence of the teacher aside, and in particular an infectious enthusiasm for his subject, there is a need for more extensive exploitation of written material. At sixth form level, there can be the critical appraisal of scientific articles and papers, especially where there is conflicting evidence. There can be reading of a book by a master of his subject with subsequent discussion between pupil and teacher. *King Solomon's Ring* or *The Double Helix* are typical illustrations. Then there are classics of scientific literature such as Darwin's *Essay of 1844* on the theory of evolution. Science fiction, including classics like *1984* and *Brave New World* may allow pupils to explore and discuss imaginative possibilities which are scientifically well-founded.

Club activities and outside speakers are important. To have a good speaker from the local university, polytechnic or industry, who transmits his scholarship and enthusiasm to science clubs, will often help individual pupils who show a keen interest in the speaker's field. Such a person opens windows too, to new interests. Universities can be very helpful with exceptional pupils. Secondment of bright children to industry, or to further or higher education in the holidays to work in the laboratories of gifted scientists are possibilities worthy of consideration as opportunities for exposure to research resources. If a school is fortunate, a teacher with research interests can help to spark off critical enquiry in gifted (and other) pupils. The Royal Society scheme for research by school teachers in their schools is an imaginative one and has paid dividends in fostering pupil interest in science.

Finally, there is a need to temper the interests of gifted science pupils in both main school and the sixth form, with sufficient breadth of study. Science sixth formers often have narrow interests. If allowed they tend to choose more science in general studies options: electronics, photography, astronomy, heredity, rather than compensatory elements. A balanced framework for all sixth formers is necessary so that mixed arts/science groups can discuss together aspects of the major areas of human experience—scientific and mathematical as well as literary, historical and aesthetic. Tony, described earlier, could become narrow and specialised if allowed. Later on his working decisions might be made without any reference to aesthetic, social or moral criteria. Foundations for value judgement of the place of science in society should be laid at school.

12   Technology

Signs of technological giftedness

Technologists rarely pursue perfection in any absolute sense. Unlike so many fields of human endeavour, the manifestation of giftedness is not excellence in one field but excellence in compromise. For example, the problem of how 'best' to span a river will not, indeed cannot, be solved by building a perfect bridge, but rather by building a bridge which will take into account the length of time building will take, the estimated working load and life span, the cost and availability of materials, the state of knowledge in bridge building, the size and skill of the workforce, the aesthetic appearance of the product and the social and environmental consequences of the new structure. What may be an optimum solution for spanning the Humber will be quite different from that for spanning a stream in the grounds of a primary school.

A second difficulty emerges when identifying technological giftedness. Technology is concerned with the control of our material world. Beyond an understanding of control concepts and principles, there is no essential body of knowledge which must be mastered, no essential practical skill to be practised to perfection, for these will vary with the task. But there are cognitive skills and modes of working which are present in any problem-solving activity in which a human need is met by the appropriate use of human and material resources. It is these cognitive skills, plus certain dispositions, which enable teachers to say with some assurance that they can spot gifted children who may become gifted technologists. The marks which identify the child include:

i. Eagerness to accept a challenge of using existing knowledge or skills to meet a human need or overcome a practical problem. Gifted children rarely await a challenge; rather they actively seek to deploy their resources of knowledge and skill as they require them.

This eagerness is often accompanied by quiet confidence. One teacher accustomed to teaching able youngsters commented that what distinguished the gifted technologist was this confidence in finding a solution to the apparently insoluble.

ii. Patience to plan an approach to a problem, rather than rushing into the first line of empirical solution. A gifted child puts time and effort into researching the background to a problem, into collecting data and considering possible approaches, into planning his/her time and effort.

iii. Capacity to take into account the interaction between several factors in a problem and to think of them as parts of a system. Much of the school content is taught, if not acquired, in a simplistic and linear fashion. One step follows another. Technological problems are rarely so simple. Several variables may need to be considered together.

iv. The willingness to acquire new skills and knowledge which could lead to a more effective or efficient solution. For example, by learning to join materials by unfamiliar techniques, or by studying electronic circuitry.

In one school, a project was held up by the consistent failure of a coupling between an engine and a shaft. After persistent attempts to avoid disintegration of the coupling when the engine ran at high speed, one boy decided to investigate the failure by high-speed photography—a technique of which he had no knowledge. He read extensively on the topic of high-speed photography, borrowed a suitable camera, made tests and produced photographs which gave clues which led to the eventual modification of the coupling.

v. A disposition to model a solution before commencing work. The model can be graphic, three dimensional or conceptual, as in mathematical modelling. Modelling serves to show the interaction between complex relationships. It serves to reduce a system to its essential elements, or it may serve to rehearse the stages through which an artefact moves during construction.

vi. Creativeness in the sense of being able to generate more than one solution to a problem, and of seeing that existing knowledge and skills have relevance in novel situations. The gifted technologist is inventive and capable of thinking outside convention.

In one school, a teacher asked pupils to drive model vehicles as far across a room as they could using a hairdryer as 'wind' source. Most pupils devised sails to mount on the vehicles as the obvious line of approach. Two boys adopted quite a different approach. They built a propeller-driven windlass which, when turned by the airflow from the dryer, very effectively hauled their model right across the room.

vii. Capacity to select and to follow an optimum course of action, recognising that there must be a 'trade-off' between various solutions. Sometimes a simple solution may be all that is required.

In one school, a group of boys were given the problem of raising tin cans from the floor to bench level. One group devised a simple see saw, one end of which could be trodden on to flick the cans upward. The solution was simple, fast, cheap and effective and avoided the time consuming activity of building cranes, lifts or pulley systems.

viii. Communication skills of a high order. The technologist at school and at work may be taking lines of action which are not conventional or standard practice. Teacher, employer, or man in the street may demand explanation. This is usually in graphic form, since this is the simplest way to convey a picture of a proposed artefact, or system. Technologists often work in teams, where again, efficient communication of intent and direction of progress is of high importance.

ix. Awareness of the social consequences of 'solving' a technological problem. At school or at work, the aesthetic effects of an artefact, the physical hazards which accompany its use, or any other adverse side effects are considerations which the gifted technologist embodies in his general ability to grasp interactions inside and outside the physical system he is seeking to modify.

Examples of technologically gifted children

Peter, a sixth former, working with a science teacher noted the crude way in which his local garage tested car brakes, and decided to devise a 'decelerometer' to measure braking efficiency. He considered a variety of solutions based upon pendulums, rolling balls, strain gauges and sliding weights and in each case made models and illustrations which he discussed with his teachers. He built a prototype and spent considerable time exploring various ways of calibrating the device. He had a good grounding in physics but acquired new practical skills as they were needed. The whole project was carefully documented and illustrated so that he could enter into dialogue with the teacher. Finally it was tested, evaluated by the pupil and an improved Mark 2 version was produced.

Paul, a fourth year pupil in an inner city comprehensive had no interest or apparent aptitude for any work in the fourth year curriculum; he was a trouble maker who only desired to leave school. The school placed him in a group which was carrying out some trials upon some curriculum development material in control technology. Paul's interest was fired and it became apparent to the teacher that he had above average capacity to think divergently. The course demanded that simple knowledge of structures, electrical and electronic principles could be used to solve open-ended problems. Although he remained somewhat taciturn, he tackled increasingly difficult problems of control, using kits and electronic components to make machines to detect changes, transport objects, sort small components into different boxes, or devise alarm systems. Possibly the verbally based, traditionally taught curriculum was of little interest and challenge to him, giving few opportunities for the exercise of his technological characteristics. But the control technology course may have afforded him the outlet which enabled his gifts to be identified. Paul remained at school beyond the minimum school leaving age, took GCE examinations and eventually followed a career in engineering.

Sometimes individual giftedness is difficult to detect, for so often technological projects in school are team exercises. For example, two schools in different parts of the country have had small teams of children working on problems of written communication which are experienced by people with severe physical handicap. Both schools had mixed teams of four pupils which, after careful planning, research of the basic problem, visits to handicapped people, and acquisition of new skills, succeeded in modifying conventional typewriters to respond to one imprecise muscular movement.

Identifying and providing for the gifted

Since the move to introduce technology into the secondary school curriculum became more marked some ten years ago, teachers have argued that several factors are working against the effective identification of and provision for the gifted technologist.

First, the gifted all-rounder (like Peter) is likely to be steered away from 'practical subjects' towards the conventional 'academically respectable' subjects at O- and A-level. Some technology teachers bitterly attack engineering departments in universities for calling for A-level mathematics and physics and neglecting to see that these subjects embody few of the qualities listed above.

Secondly, the 'hidden' technologist, such as Paul, may be a child who never encounters teaching method or content which can reveal his talent. He may be fed on diet of subject orientated material taught in a didactic manner. The discovery of Paul came late in his school life. One wonders how many youngsters pass undiscovered in a curriculum based on verbal knowledge.

Thirdly, in a crowded curriculum, there may be no space for a subject labelled 'technology', and instead there may have to be reliance upon a technological flavour being present in science, craft, or the social studies. To some extent this does happen, notably in craft workshops where the smaller group size, greater freedom from prescribed subject matter and the strong design methodology are factors which encourage the emergence of gifted technologists. Project work in science is another curricular area where the characteristics of technological behaviour readily find expression. Yet to rely upon existing subjects to develop and support the characteristics is not entirely satisfactory. It means that technology must be taught by teachers who have other important aims to pursue, such as the pursuit of excellence in craft or truth in science, who are trained for their own discipline and who have to meet the requirements of their own examinations. Those who would teach technology, in science for example, must consider what content and method is at the risk of being displaced, what alternative examinations are acceptable, and where and when they acquire their additional training.

These problems notwithstanding, craft and science teachers have made considerable efforts to introduce technological content and to modify examinations to test technological characteristics. Particularly commendable are CSE Mode 3 examinations which call for the solution of practical projects in technology. Frequently they pose design briefs, evaluate by continuous assessment which calls for evidence of searching for data, posing various solutions to the design and effective planning and executing of a work schedule.

A minority of heads have established technology courses within the curriculum. Usually these are fourth year options, but a few schools regard 'technological literacy' as a core curriculum subject (this is compulsory in Belgian, French, Italian and some German schools) and offer technology to all pupils lower in the school. Where this is done, the girls with technological gifts have the rare opportunity to show their talents—an opportunity which in general is denied. Where technology is one of several options in the upper school it again faces the problem of competing for the time of the gifted all-rounder who is wooed away to A-level examinations in the traditional academic mould.

Despite difficulties of identification and course provision, the picture within courses is one of good quality. Gradually teachers are retraining to teach technology. LEAs, the DES, the Open University, and the National Centre for School Technology have offered in-service courses in School Technology. Curricular development materials are now on the market, where few existed a decade ago. Technology teachers are among the more sophisticated and perceptive of project method teachers. Local and national support systems exist in the form of local science and technology centres, the National Centre for School Technology and the School Technology Forum. There is a Standing Conference on School Science and Technology which has representatives from industry, educational administration and teaching.

Examinations are changing to take account of some of the characteristics listed at the outset. CSE examinations in technology have already been mentioned. One A-level engineering science syllabus aims to test, not so much specific knowledge but a pupil's capability to: 'Design the manner in which an optimum solution may be obtained efficiently and to propose alternative solutions, taking into account the restraints imposed by material, economic and social considerations'.

In short, the provision for technology in schools, though meagre, is of good quality, and well able to support the gifted.

What still needs to be done?

Clearly, from the analysis above, there is not yet enough pressure from the public, from industry and from higher education (particularly from engineering faculties in universities) to identify the characteristics of a gifted technologist. For example, insufficient work has been done to identify the behavioural characteristics displayed by the talented engineer. Without public awareness and pressure, there can be little possibility of making curricular space.

Although in-service provision for would-be technology teachers exists, and sound curricular materials are available, teachers in initial training are technologically illiterate. A mere handful of courses in technology are to be found in colleges of education.

Because of the shortage of technology teachers, heads sometimes seek to encourage interdisciplinary work or project work with a technological flavour. In one school, a well-intentioned head had been able to timetable for project work, but many of the staff had neither a grasp of the nature of project method nor sufficient training or insight into the nature of technology.

Given that curricular space can be found and that the characteristics of gifted technological behaviour are identified, two more things need to happen. First, technological behaviour needs to be divorced from technological artefacts. That is to say, the emphasis upon the actual product which is sometimes seen in project competitions and school open days needs to be supplemented by evidence of the quality of thinking, the extent of research, and the variety and validity of solutions by individual pupils. The second related point is that more recognition of this evidence, in the form of examination syllabuses, employers' tests and university entrance boards, needs to be encapsulated into our educational system.

Printed in England for Her Majesty's Stationery Office
by Burgess & Son (Abingdon) Ltd
Dd 586775   K64 6/77